FANTASY

CROSS STITCH

60 SPELL-BINDING DESIGNS

LESLEY TEARE

D&C
David and Charles

For Lynn, happy memories

A DAVID & CHARLES BOOK

David & Charles is an F+W Publications Inc. company
4700 East Galbraith Road
Cincinnati, OH 45236

First published in the UK in 2008

A catalogue record for this book is available from the British Library.

ISBN-13: 978-0-7153-2689-3 hardback
ISBN-10: 0-7153-2689-9 hardback

ISBN-13: 978-0-7153-2700-5 paperback
ISBN-10: 0-7153-2700-3 paperback

Printed in China by SNP Leefung Pte Ltd
for David & Charles
Brunel House   Newton Abbot   Devon

Executive Editor Cheryl Brown
Desk Editor Bethany Dymond
Project Editor and Chart Preparation Lin Clements
Senior Designer Charly Bailey
Production Controller Ros Napper

Visit our website at www.davidandcharles.co.uk

David & Charles books are available from all good bookshops; alternatively you can contact our
Orderline on 0870 9908222 or write to us at FREEPOST EX2 110, D&C Direct, Newton Abbot, TQ12 4ZZ
(no stamp required UK only); US customers call 800-289-0963 and
Canadian customers call 800-840-5220.

Contents

Introduction

Fantasy means different things to each of us. For you, it might mean exciting myths and legends or amazing other worlds; for someone else it might conjure up images of fantastic creatures or beings with mystical powers. Since the beginning of time people have made up epic fantasy stories in the form of myths and legends to reflect their role in the universe and express their hopes and dreams. Through the ages, craftsmen and artists have used their skills and imagination to convey how we would 'see' these wonderful creations.

We are surrounded by a rich seam of fantasy inspirations, and the cross stitch designs in this book are my interpretation of some fantasy themes. Some of the images

may be familiar to you, such as the legend of the unicorn; others, like the birth totems of Native American culture, are less well known. There are impressive 'showpiece' designs and also a wealth of smaller motifs within the chapters, perfect for creating a wide range of quicker projects, such as cards, gifts and keepsakes. There are also many ideas throughout suggesting other ways you could use the designs. Many of the designs have been given additional fantasy elements by the inclusion of glittering metallic threads and gleaming seed beads.

I hope the diverse fantasy themes in this book will encourage you to escape on a series of enchanted journeys and allow you to create a little magic of your own whilst stitching these lovely designs.

The dragon has been part of fantasy folklore for centuries, inspiring art and literature. This fabulous creature looks stunning on red Aida fabric.

Spell-binding Wizard

*Do not meddle in the affairs
of wizards, for they are subtle
and quick to anger.*

(*The Lord of the Rings*, J.R.R. Tolkein)

Throughout history and across cultures there are grand tales of wizards – who has not heard of the Arthurian legends of Merlin or of Gandalf, friend to Middle Earth? Wizards have long been portrayed as masters of nature, keepers of secret knowledge, who by spells, potions and incantations can transform himself and others.

With a well-developed sense of drama, and perhaps a twinkle in his eye, this wizard is ready to demonstrate his magical powers. His richly decorated robes allude to the wonders of the universe and the zodiac. Magic dust flows from his hand to weave spells and fulfil fantasies. It cascades over the crystal ball, which glitters with mysterious omens full of fire, ready to cast more enchanting spells. From his long, pointed hat, which displays a star charm, to his pixie-style shoes, this delightful character is stitched in bright colours of reds, greens, mauves and blues. Gold threads and wonderful metallic colours sparkle from the black fabric background, bringing the character to life. A simple gold frame is all that is required to finish off this detailed design.

Wizard Picture

A wizard is a must in any book on fantasy and this character is great fun – you can almost hear him muttering his spells of incantation. With all his colourful clothes, the design is enjoyable to stitch. When using metallic threads, work with shorter lengths, about 30cm (12in).

Stitch count
219h x 186w

Design size
39.5 x 34cm
(15½ x 13¼ in)

You will need

☆ 51 x 46cm (20 x 18in)
   14-count black Aida

☆ Tapestry needle size 24

☆ DMC stranded cotton (floss)
   as listed in chart key

☆ Kreinik #4 Very Fine Braid
   as listed in chart key

☆ Framecraft star (CP910)

1 Prepare for work, referring to page 95 if necessary. Find and mark the centre of the fabric and centre of the chart on pages 10–13. For your own use you could photocopy the chart parts and tape them together. Note: some colours use more than one skein – see chart key for details. Mount your fabric in an embroidery frame if you wish.

2 Start stitching from the centre of the chart working over one block of Aida. Use two strands of stranded cotton (floss) for cross stitches and one strand for backstitches. Use one strand for all Kreinik #4 braid cross stitches. Sew on the star charm in the position shown on the chart.

3 Once all the stitching is complete, frame the design as a picture (see page 98).

Imagine this...

☆ This colourful design would make a truly impressive wall hanging, especially for a boy who is mad about magic. The black fabric emphasizes all the bright colours.

☆ The design would also make a great decoration for a sleep-over bag. Sew it to a ready-made bag as a patch.

☆ If worked on an 18-count Aida to create a smaller design size, 30.5 x 26.5cm (12 x 10½ in), the wizard would be perfect attached to the front of a journal or scrapbook.

Top left

Top right

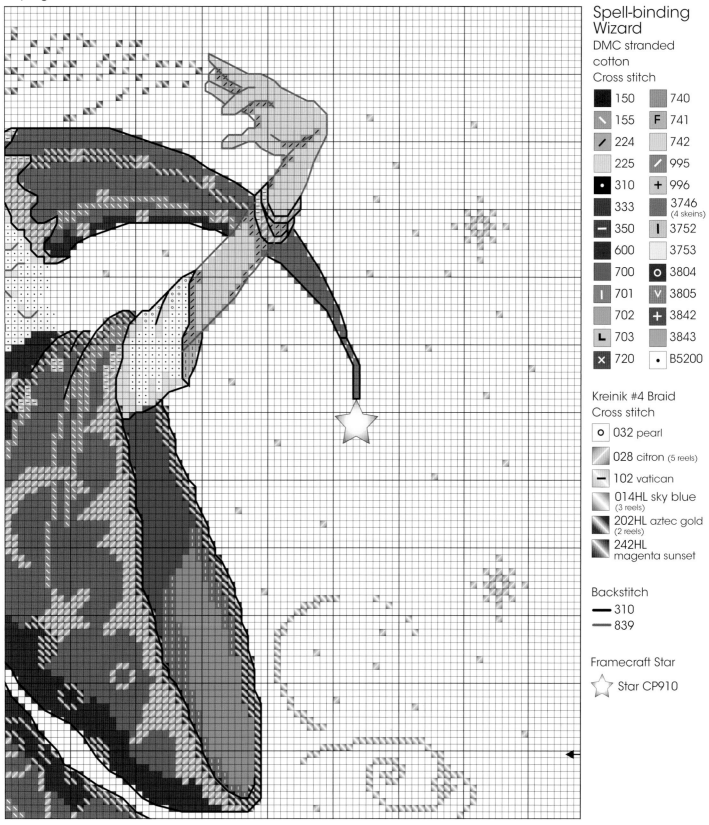

Spell-binding Wizard

DMC stranded cotton
Cross stitch

■	150	▨	740
＼	155	F	741
／	224	▨	742
▨	225	／	995
●	310	+	996
▨	333		3746 (4 skeins)
—	350	I	3752
■	600	▨	3753
▨	700	O	3804
I	701	V	3805
▨	702	+	3842
L	703	▨	3843
X	720	•	B5200

Kreinik #4 Braid
Cross stitch

O	032 pearl
▨	028 citron (5 reels)
—	102 vatican
▨	014HL sky blue (3 reels)
▨	202HL aztec gold (2 reels)
▨	242HL magenta sunset

Backstitch

— 310
— 839

Framecraft Star

☆ Star CP910

Bottom left

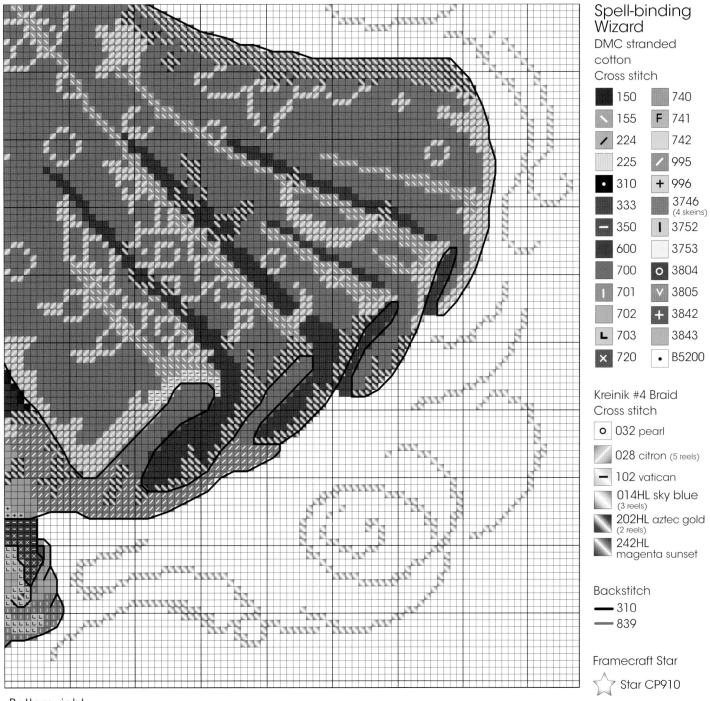

Spell-binding Wizard

DMC stranded cotton
Cross stitch

■	150	▨	740
＼	155	F	741
／	224		742
	225	／	995
•	310	+	996
▦	333		3746 (4 skeins)
−	350	I	3752
	600		3753
	700	O	3804
I	701	V	3805
	702	+	3842
L	703		3843
X	720	•	B5200

Kreinik #4 Braid
Cross stitch

O	032 pearl
	028 citron (5 reels)
−	102 vatican
	014HL sky blue (3 reels)
	202HL aztec gold (2 reels)
	242HL magenta sunset

Backstitch
— 310
— 839

Framecraft Star
☆ Star CP910

Bottom right

Spell-binding Wizard

Blue Wizard   Stitch count: 40h x 34w
Design size: 7.2 x 6cm (2¾ x 2½in)

Green Wizard   Stitch count: 46h x 34w
Design size: 8.4 x 6cm (3¼ x 2½in)

Purple Wizard   Stitch count: 52h x 43w
Design size: 9.4 x 7.6cm (3¾ x 3in)

Pink Wizard   Stitch count: 53h x 36w
Design size: 9.6 x 6cm (3¾ x 2½in)

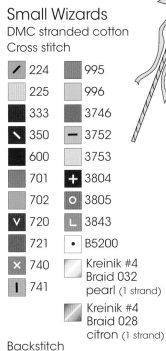

Small Wizards

DMC stranded cotton
Cross stitch

∕	224		995
	225		996
	333		3746
∖	350	−	3752
	600		3753
	701	+	3804
	702	O	3805
V	720	L	3843
	721	•	B5200
X	740		Kreinik #4 Braid 032 pearl (1 strand)
I	741		Kreinik #4 Braid 028 citron (1 strand)

Backstitch
—— 801

Imagine this. . .

☆ These little designs are great fun and perfect for quick-stitch projects such as the birthday card shown below. Write your own message with a colourful, broad-nibbed felt pen and decorate the card with stick-on stars or sequins.

☆ Any of the wizards could be stitched as a patch and sewn to a pyjama case or dressing gown.

☆ Stitch all four small wizards to make a colourful cushion for a child's bedroom.

☆ The wizard on his broomstick would make a great design for a notebook or diary cover – stitch it on a length of 7.6cm (3in) wide Aida band and attach to the book with double-sided tape.

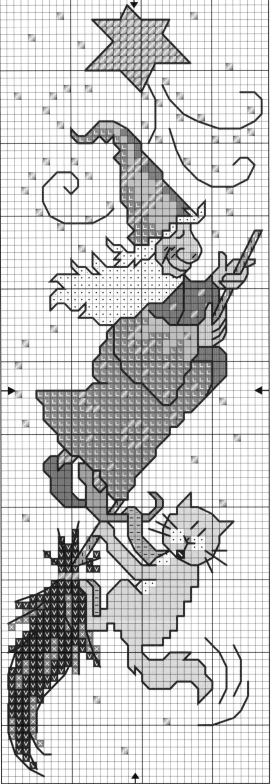

Wizard and Cat
Stitch count: 106h x 36w
Design size: 19.2 x 6.5cm (7½ x 2½in)

Song of the Mermaid

*Pale rays of light tiptoed across the waters;
and by and by there was to be heard a sound at once
the most musical and the most melancholy in the world:
the mermaids calling to the moon.*

(*The Adventures of Peter Pan*, J. M. Barrie)

Tales of mermaids have been told for centuries and form a large part of seafaring lore, especially around coastal areas. Their sighting was thought to be a bad omen for sailors, foretelling storms and rough seas. The mermaid derives her name from the middle-English word 'mere', which means sea. Legend tells of a creature swimming through the surf, calling men into the sea. A mermaid has been described as a beautiful woman from the waist up with a glistening fish tail below – an image that has inspired artists and poets from earliest times.

My image of a mermaid is a beautiful maiden watching her entourage of pretty water babies bringing gifts of a shell, whilst colourful fish and seahorses swim around them. This picture is stitched in all the colours of the sea and with the addition of beautiful metallic threads and shimmering beads it depicts a fairytale world deep in the ocean.

The design would look beautiful made into a cushion or a wall hanging, or choose some of the smaller fish and seahorses to stitch on Aida bands for bathroom accessories.

Mermaid Picture

This delightful group of mermaid, cute water babies and accompanying fish is stitched in soft watery colours on a pale sea-green fabric. The design could also be stitched over two threads of 28-count linen. There are also some smaller motifs that could be quickly stitched for a variety of projects (see pages 24 and 25 for ideas and the charts).

Stitch count
185h x 183w

Design size
33.5 x 33cm
(13¼ x 13in)

You will need

☆ 51 x 51cm (20 x 20in) 14-count pale sea green Aida (Zweigart code 6150)

☆ Tapestry needle size 24 and a beading needle

☆ DMC stranded cotton (floss) as listed in the chart key

☆ Kreinik #4 Very Fine Braid as listed in the chart key

☆ Mill Hill glass seed beads as listed in the chart key

☆ Suitable picture frame

1 Prepare for work, referring to page 95 if necessary. Find and mark the centre of the fabric and centre of the chart on pages 20–23. For your own use you could photocopy the chart parts and tape them together. Note: some colours use more than one reel of Kreinik – see chart key for details. Mount your fabric in an embroidery frame if you wish.

2 Start stitching from the centre of the chart and fabric, working over one block of Aida. Use two strands of stranded cotton (floss) for full and three-quarter cross stitches and one strand for backstitches. Use one strand for all Kreinik #4 braid cross stitches. Attach the beads where indicated on the chart, using a beading needle and matching thread (see page 97).

3 Once all the stitching is complete, frame the design as a picture (see page 98).

The designs charted on pages 24–25 ➡ *are perfect for decorating small projects. Here, two have been used to adorn a bath towel and a ready-made towelling bag. Use two strands of thread for cross stitch and one for backstitch. The towel design was stitched on 14-count white Aida band and sewn on to the towel. The bag has the design worked on an Aida patch with frayed edges, attached to the bag with iron-on interfacing (see page 99). See charts for stitch counts and design sizes.*

Who would be a mermaid fair,
singing alone, combing her hair,
Under the sea in a golden curl
with a comb of pearl on a throne?

(Alfred Lord Tennyson)

Top left

Song of the Mermaid

DMC stranded cotton
Cross stitch

▪ 310	F 702	N 745	z 950	× 3799
434	703	746	958	⁄ 3812
L 435	+ 729	772	H 959	I 3823
436	738	− 807	964	\ 3853
⁄ 437	⅄ 739	819	o 3064	T 3854
∧ 676	742	o 3064		⁄
I 700	S 743	↑ 920	3765	▪ blanc
701	744	V 921	U 3766	
701	744	938	\ 3774	

Kreinik #4 Braid
Cross stitch (1 strand)

⁄ 015 chartreuse	
027 orange (5 reels)	
− 127 yellow orange (3 reels)	
\ 684 aquamarine (2 reels)	
⁄ 1432 blue ice (2 reels)	
⁄ 9192 light peach (2 reels)	

Backstitch

— 310	
— 356	
— 433	
— 3064	
— Kreinik #4 braid 051HL sapphire	

Mill Hill
Seed Beads

○ 00479 pearl	
○ 00561 pale green	
○ 02031 lime	

Bottom left

Song of the Mermaid
DMC stranded cotton
Cross stitch

• 310	F 702	N 745	Z 950	× 3799
■ 434	703	746	958	╱ 3812
L 435	+ 729	772	H 959	I 3823
436	738	− 807	964	╲ 3853
╱ 437	⋏ 739	819	o 3064	T 3854
⋀ 676	742	↑ 920	3765	• blanc
I 700	S 743	V 921	U 3766	
701	744	938	╲ 3774	

Kreinik #4 Braid
Cross stitch (1 strand)

╱ 015 chartreuse	
╲ 027 orange (5 reels)	
− 127 yellow orange (3 reels)	
╱ 684 aquamarine (2 reels)	
╱ 1432 blue ice (2 reels)	
╱ 9192 light peach (2 reels)	

Backstitch

—	310
—	356
—	433
—	3064
—	Kreinik #4 braid 051HL sapphire

Mill Hill
Seed Beads

◯	00479 pearl
◉	00561 pale green
◉	02031 lime

Bottom right

Fish   Stitch count: 24h x 30w
Design size: 4.4 x 5.4cm (1¾ x 2⅛in)

Seahorses Stitch count: 37h x 32w
Design size: 6.7 x 5.8cm (2¾ x 2¼in)

Sea Dragon   Stitch count: 19h x 41w
Design size: 3.5 x 7.5cm (1½ x 3in)

Dolphin
Stitch count: 41h x 44w
Design size: 7.5 x 8cm
(3 x 3⅛in)

Babies   Stitch count: 39h x 17w
Design size: 7 x 3cm (2¾ x 1¼in)

Mermaid   Stitch count: 38h x 18w
Design size: 7 x 3cm (2¾ x 1¼in)

Lotus   Stitch count: 34h x 36w
Design size: 6.2 x 6.5cm (2½ x 2½in)

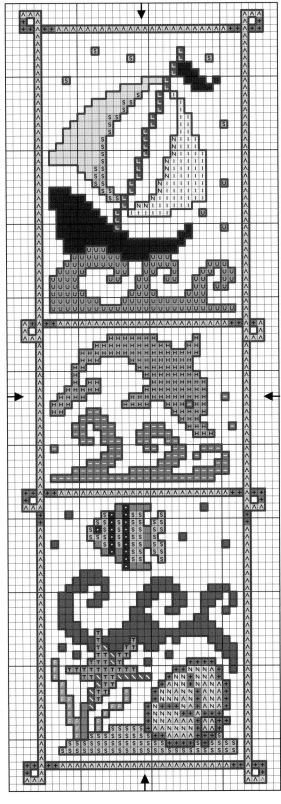

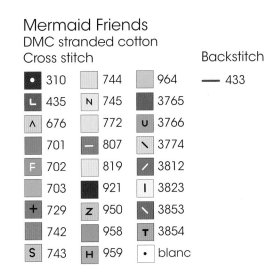

Mermaid Friends
DMC stranded cotton
Cross stitch   Backstitch

● 310	744	964	── 433
L 435	N 745	3765
∧ 676	772	U 3766
701	─ 807	＼ 3774
F 702	819	／ 3812
703	921	I 3823
+ 729	Z 950	＼ 3853
742	958	T 3854
S 743	H 959	● blanc

Imagine this...

☆ The designs charted here are perfect for decorating small projects, such as the towel and bag shown on page 18. You could also use smaller motifs from the main chart, either alone or repeated to form borders.

☆ The larger designs would make very pretty pictures, perhaps framed similarly and displayed as a group.

☆ The fish and seahorse motifs would be ideal for someone who enjoys keeping fish – perhaps to decorate the front of a journal or notebook.

☆ The small fish and seahorse motifs could be stitched for key rings or a set of coasters.

All at Sea
Stitch count: 105h x 34w
Design size: 19 x 6.2cm (7½ x 2½in)

Native American Birth Totems

*Certain things catch your eye,
but pursue only those that capture your heart.*

(Old Indian saying)

The word 'totem' means emblem or sign and Native American beliefs identify certain animals and birds as totems, which are spiritually symbolic. Each of the twelve phases of the moon has an associated animal or bird and your birth totem can tell you many things about your personality, your attitudes, your strengths and weaknesses.

The twelve birth totems are linked to the four elements of Fire, Air, Earth and Water. The Elemental Clan into which you are born represents the element you relate to and share characteristics with. The Thunderbird Clan element is Fire, the Butterfly is Air, the Turtle is Earth and the Frog is Water.

I have used these birth totems as inspiration for an unusual alternative to the astrological zodiac seen in the Queen of the Night chapter (page 64). Each totem (four of which are shown opposite) has its own plant and phase of the moon, which are represented in the design. The four clan signs and the twelve birth totems have been stitched on Rustico Aida because its natural, flecked appearance complements the designs perfectly.

Elemental Clans

These little elemental clan signs are perfect for greetings cards and gift tags. They are stitched on 14-count Rustico Aida but could also be worked over two threads of 28-count linen.

Stitch count
33h x 33w (for each design)

Design size
6 x 6cm (2⅜ x 2⅜in)

You will need (for each design)
☆ 15 x 15cm (6 x 6in) 14-count Rustico Aida

☆ Tapestry needle size 24

☆ DMC stranded cotton (floss) as listed in the chart key

☆ Suitable picture frame or card mount

1 Prepare for work, referring to page 95 if necessary. Mark the centre of the fabric and the centre of the chart (page 33). Use an embroidery frame if you wish.

2 Start stitching from the centre of the fabric and chart, working outwards. Work the full and three-quarter stitches using two strands of stranded cotton. Work the backstitches with one strand.

3 Once all stitching is complete, mount in a suitable frame or card (see page 98 or 100 for advice).

Birth Totems

Use these twelve charming designs (shown over the next four pages) not only for framed pictures but for beautiful cards that a recipient will love to keep. The borders are interchangeable but they can also be omitted – useful if the design needs to fit into a specific card aperture. The designs could also be stitched over two threads of 28-count linen.

Stitch count
79h x 51w (for each design, maximum)

Design size
14.3 x 9.2cm (5½ x 3½in)

You will need (for each design)
☆ 25 x 20cm (10 x 8in) 14-count Rustico Aida

☆ Tapestry needle size 24

☆ DMC stranded cotton (floss) as listed in the chart key

☆ Suitable picture frame or card mount

1 Prepare your fabric. Stitch the designs using the charts on pages 34–41. Work outwards from the centre of the fabric and centre of the chart, using two strands of stranded cotton for full and three-quarter cross stitches and French knots and one strand for the backstitches.

2 Once all stitching is complete, frame the design as a picture or make up in another way of your choice.

Thunderbird Clan

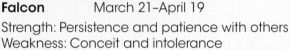

Element: Fire

Thunderbird (hawk) clan people are doers, often leaders and are usually in the spotlight, expressing all their feelings. They seem to need the energy of Fire in all its forms to strengthen and renew the fire that is always within them.

Falcon   March 21–April 19

Strength: Persistence and patience with others
Weakness: Conceit and intolerance

Falcon people are observant, spontaneous and uncomplicated but can lose sight of the bigger picture. They are very open, direct and honest and thanks to their down-to-earth charm are very endearing.

Owl   November 23–December 21

Strength: optimistic, happy and focused
Weakness: Overbearing, often exaggerates

Owl people have an enduring strength that allows them to follow their high ideals and formidable goals. They are lively, self-reliant, with an eye for detail. They strive for a deeper understanding and a more profound truth.

Salmon   July 22–August 21

Strength: Tolerance, humbleness and letting go
Weakness: Egotistical and controlling nature

Salmon people are enthusiastic and self-confident, make good protectors and are willing and able to lead. They are, however, uncompromising and forceful, and can seem a little arrogant. They are easily hurt by neglect.

Butterfly Clan

Element: Air

Butterfly Clan people are always active
– physically, mentally and emotionally. They
have new ideas and unexpected ways of doing
things, and like Air, are always changing. They
enjoy being outside in big, open spaces and
have their best inspirations then.

Otter   January 20–February 18

Strength: Inventive, soothing and very perceptive
Weakness: Nosy, unpredictable, often too blunt

Otters are friendly, lively, sociable and perceptive.
They can be revolutionaries and rebels, but are still
co-operative and able to positively influence team
spirit. Friendship and solidarity are important to them.

Deer   May 21–June 20

Strength: Persistence and concentration
Weakness: Restless and insecure

Deer people are very sensitive but also relaxed
and carefree. They are open-minded and
intellectually awake, loathe routine and enjoy
variety and challenges. They have a wild side,
often leaping without reflection.

Raven   September 22–October 22

Strength: Caution, making decisions and letting go
Weakness: Taking sides, indecision, trusting too much

Ravens dislike solitude. Although usually pleasant
and good-natured, they are affected by negative
atmospheres, becoming gloomy and prickly.
Harmonious and peaceful interaction is important,
making them diplomatic and accommodating.

Frog Clan

Element: Water

People of the Frog Clan have deep, easily flowing feelings, which enable them to bring fresh new feelings into any project, flushing away stalemates and obstacles. Water is a healing element and Frog people have a natural gift for healing and empathy.

Wolf February 19–March 20

Strength: Sensitivity
Weakness: Laziness, easily influenced

Wolves are sensitive, artistic and intuitive people to whom others turn for help. They value freedom and their own space and are easily affected by others. They are philosophical, trusting and genuine but their good nature can be misused.

Woodpecker June 21–July 21

Strength: Tender and sympathetic
Weakness: Moody, often unforgiving

Woodpeckers (flickers) are sensitive and empathic people who depend on their emotions. They protect their boundaries until they can trust people and situations. They reach deep into their psyche, creating happiness as well as chaos.

Snake October 23–November 22

Strength: Discerning and imaginative
Weakness: Mistrustful and often stubborn

Snakes are secretive and mysterious, hiding their feelings beneath coolness. Adaptable and imaginative, they can bounce back from tough situations. They are competitive and persistent but their support can be counted on.

Turtle Clan

Element: Earth

People of the Turtle clan tend to be brave, loyal, stubborn, methodical and practical. They have determination, but take things one step at a time. Some tend to be hard as rocks, but Turtle clan people, like the Earth, personify roots, growth and stability.

Beaver   April 20–May 20

Strength: Compassion, inner security and confidence
Weakness: Possessiveness and inflexibility

Practical and steady, Beavers have a capacity for perseverance. They are good homemakers, warm and affectionate but need harmony and peace to avoid becoming irritable. They have a keen aesthetic sense.

Bear   August 22–September 21

Strength: Optimism, tolerance and self acceptance
Weakness: Fault finding and putting things off

People born under this sign are hard working, practical and self reliant. They do not like change, preferring to stick to what is familiar. They have a flair for fixing things, are good natured and make good friends.

Snow Goose   December 22–January 19

Strength: Sociable, well spoken
Weakness: Self-doubt, can't see the forest for trees

Goose people are far-sighted idealists who are willing to explore the unknown. They approach life with enthusiasm, determined to fulfil their dreams. They are perfectionists and can appear unduly serious.

Thunderbird Clan

Turtle Clan

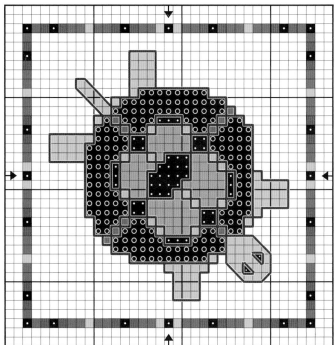

Frog Clan

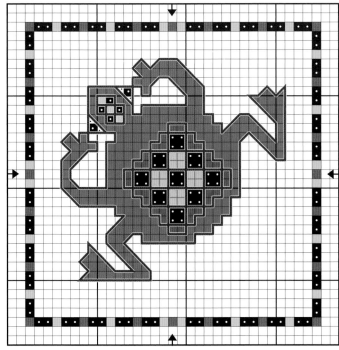

Butterfly Clan

Elemental Clans
DMC stranded cotton
Cross stitch

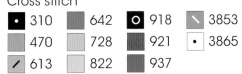

■ 310	642	◉ 918	⧄ 3853
470	728	921	• 3865
⁄ 613	822	937	

Backstitch
— 898

The individual designs do
not use all of the colours

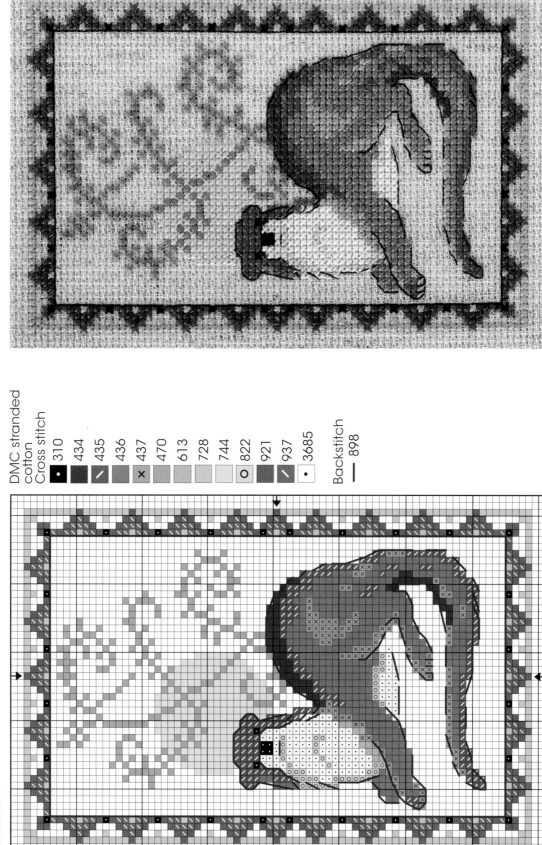

DMC stranded
cotton
Cross stitch

●	310
	434
/	435
	436
✕	437
	470
	613
	728
	744
○	822
	921
/	937
●	3685

Backstitch
— 898

Otter (Butterfly Clan)   January 20 – February 18
Cleansing Moon
Plant: Fern

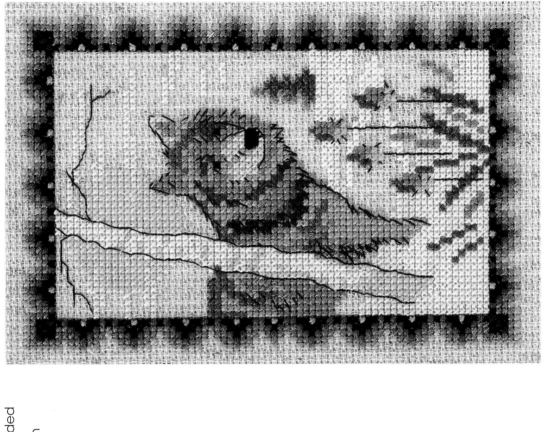

DMC stranded cotton Cross stitch

●	310	
>	433	
	434	
/	435	
	436	
	470	
	472	
–	613	
	642	
	728	
	744	
○	822	
+	918	
	921	
\	937	
	3072	
I	3756	
•	3865	

Backstitch
— 898
— 921

Wolf (Frog Clan)   February 19 – March 20
Big Winds Moon
Plant: Plantain

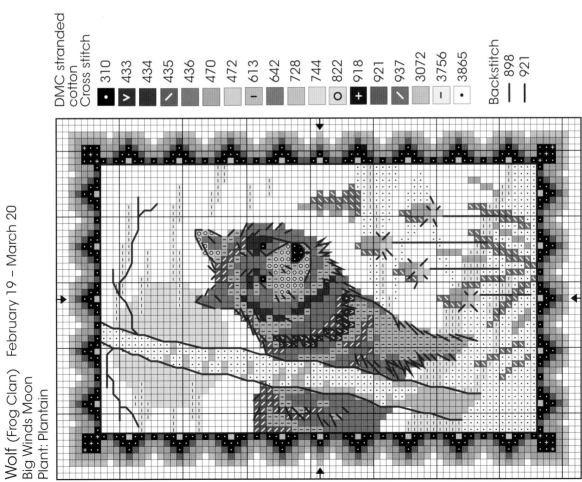

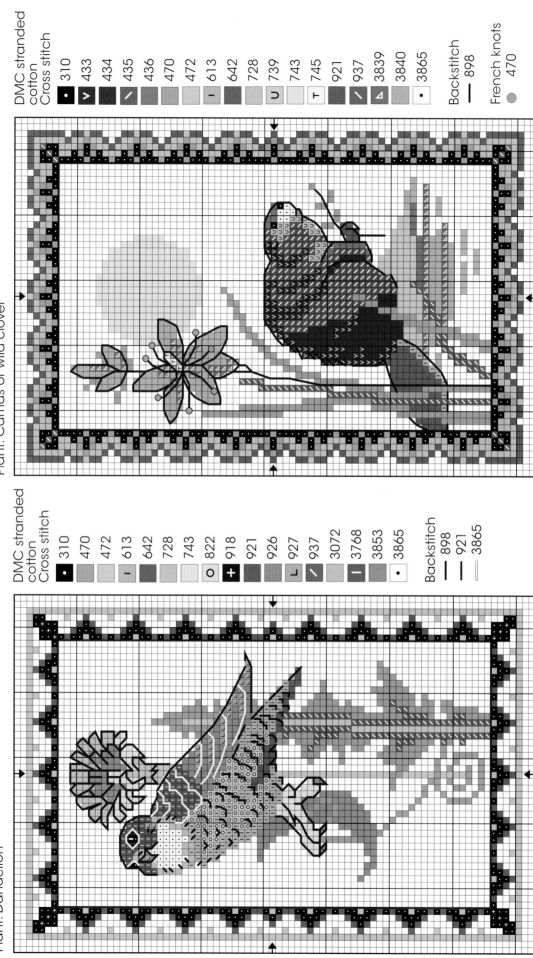

Beaver (Turtle Clan)   April 20 – May 20
Frogs Returning Moon
Plant: Camas or wild clover

DMC stranded cotton
Cross stitch

310	433
434	435
436	470
472	613
642	728
739	743
745	921
937	3839
3840	3865

Backstitch
— 898

French knots
● 470

Falcon (Thunderbird Clan)   March 21 – April 19
Budding Tree Moon
Plant: Dandelion

DMC stranded cotton
Cross stitch

310	470
472	613
642	728
743	822
918	921
926	927
937	3072
3768	3853
3865	

Backstitch
— 898
— 921
— 3865

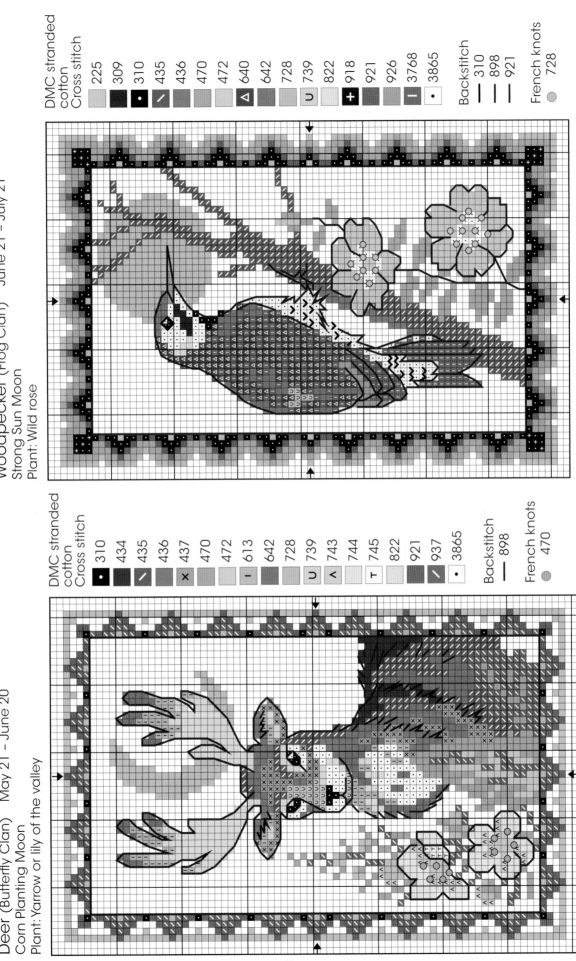

Woodpecker (Frog Clan)   June 21 – July 21
Strong Sun Moon
Plant: Wild rose

DMC stranded cotton
Cross stitch

225	
309	
310	•
435	/
436	
470	
472	
640	◁
642	
728	
739	∪
822	
918	+
921	
926	
3768	—
3865	•

Backstitch
—— 310
—— 898
—— 921

French knots
◉ 728

Deer (Butterfly Clan)   May 21 – June 20
Corn Planting Moon
Plant: Yarrow or lily of the valley

DMC stranded cotton
Cross stitch

310	•
434	
435	/
436	
437	×
470	
472	
613	—
642	
728	
739	∪
743	∧
744	
745	T
822	
921	
937	/
3865	•

Backstitch
—— 898

French knots
◉ 470

37

Bear (Turtle Clan)   August 22 – September 21
Harvest Moon
Plant: Violet

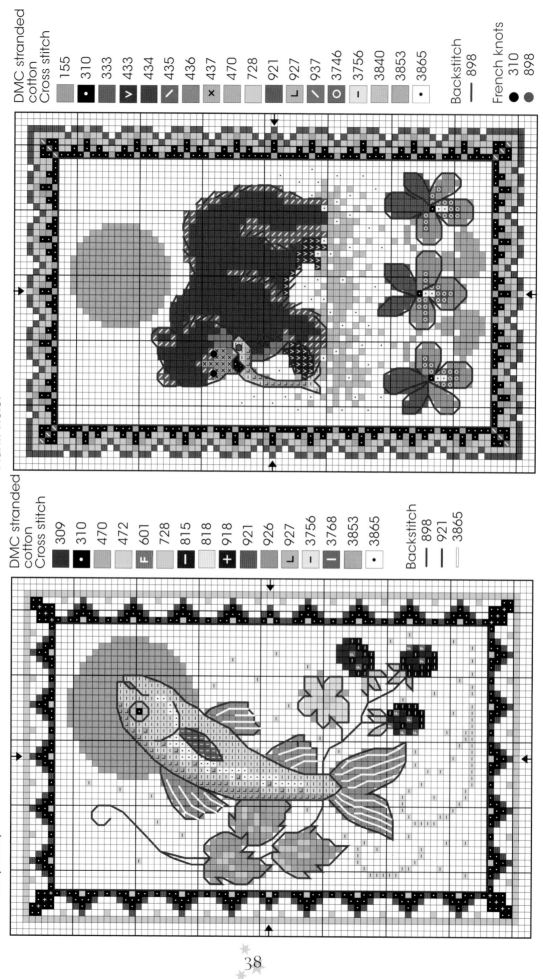

DMC stranded cotton
Cross stitch

155		
310	•	
333		
433	V	
434		
435	/	
436		
437	×	
470		
728		
921		
927	L	
937	/	
3746	O	
3756	I	
3840		
3853		
3865	•	

Backstitch
— 898

French knots
● 310
● 898

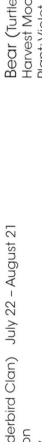

Salmon (Thunderbird Clan)   July 22 – August 21
Ripe Berries Moon
Plant: Raspberry

DMC stranded cotton
Cross stitch

309		
310	•	
470		
472		
601	F	
728		
815	I	
818		
918	+	
921		
926		
927	L	
3756	I	
3768	I	
3853		
3865	•	

Backstitch
— 898
— 921
— 3865

38

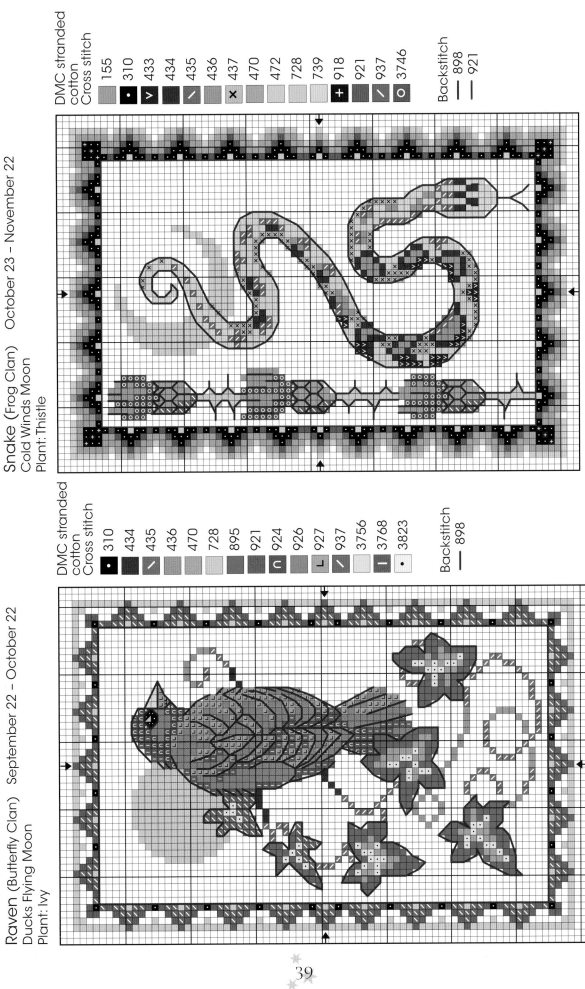

Snake (Frog Clan)   October 23 – November 22
Cold Winds Moon
Plant: Thistle

DMC stranded cotton
Cross stitch

	155
•	310
V	433
	434
/	435
	436
×	437
	470
	472
	728
	739
+	918
	921
/	937
O	3746

Backstitch
— 898
— 921

Raven (Butterfly Clan)   September 22 – October 22
Ducks Flying Moon
Plant: Ivy

DMC stranded cotton
Cross stitch

•	310
	434
/	435
	436
	470
	728
	895
	921
⊃	924
	926
⌐	927
/	937
	3756
—	3768
•	3823

Backstitch
— 898

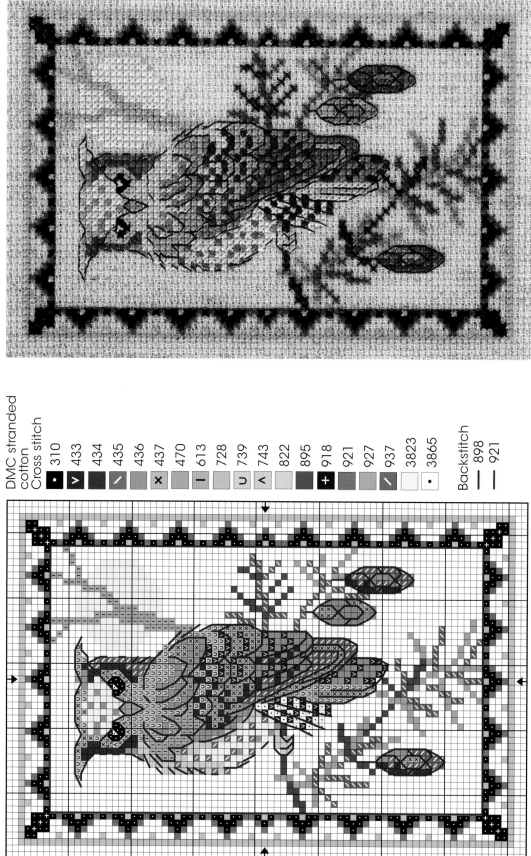

Owl (Thunderbird Clan)   November 23 – December 21
Long Snows Moon
Plant: Black spruce

DMC stranded cotton

Cross stitch

•	310
>	433
	434
/	435
	436
×	437
	470
−	613
	728
∪	739
<	743
	822
	895
+	918
	921
	927
/	937
	3823
•	3865

Backstitch
—— 898
—— 921

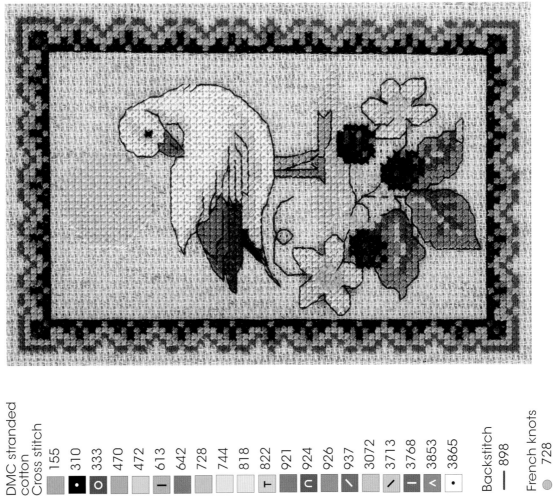

Snow Goose (Turtle Clan)   December 22 – January 19
New Moon
Plant: Bramble

DMC stranded
cotton
Cross stitch

	155
•	310
○	333
	470
	472
−	613
	642
	728
	744
	818
⊤	822
	921
∪	924
∕	926
	937
╱	3072
∣	3713
∖	3768
∨	3853
•	3865

Backstitch
— 898

French knots
● 728

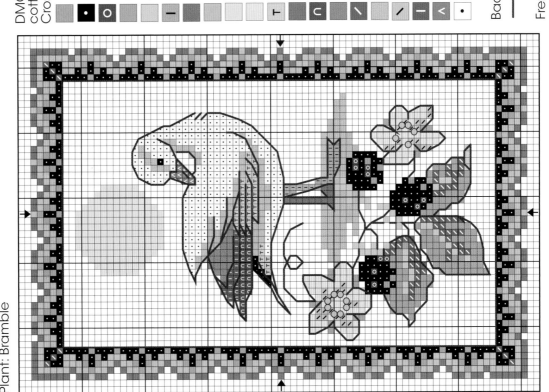

Legend of the Unicorn

All of the beasts obeyed Noah when he admitted them into the ark – all but the unicorn. Confident of his strength he boasted, 'I shall swim!'

(from a Ukrainian folktale)

The story concludes that for 40 days and nights the rains poured down, the oceans boiled and all the heights were flooded. The birds clung to the ark and when it pitched they were engulfed but the unicorn kept swimming. When the birds emerged again they perched on his horn and he went under – and that is why there are no unicorns now.

The unicorn has been a topic of wonder and speculation for centuries, glorified in poems, songs and folktales. Most cultures agree that this mystical creature had a single horn in the middle of its forehead. The word 'unicorn' comes from the Latin 'uni', meaning one, and 'cornu', meaning horn. The power and purity of the unicorn meant that its horn was considered highly magical and worth more than its weight in gold. Legend says it is impossible to capture a unicorn by force; only a gentle maiden can approach him.

The Ukrainian folktale was the inspiration for my design, showing the proud unicorn amid a whirl of wild sea foam. A dark fabric was chosen to accentuate all the gleaming silvers, whites and icy blues, with metallic threads adding an extra magical element.

Unicorn Picture

The design shows this magnificent creature prancing amid the sea foam, the shimmering movement further enhanced by tiny glass beads. Additional mythical beasts have been charted on pages 52–53, with ideas on using them.

Stitch count
192h x 224w

Design size
33 x 40cm (13 x 16in)

You will need

☆ 46 x 53cm (18 x 21in) 28-count blue Linda, (Zweigart code 560)

☆ Tapestry needle size 24 and a beading needle

☆ DMC stranded cotton (floss) as listed in chart key

☆ Kreinik #4 Very Fine Braid as listed in chart key

☆ Mill Hill glass seed beads 00479 pearly white

☆ Mill Hill petite beads 40479 pearl

Legend of the Unicorn - chart parts

1 Prepare for work, referring to page 95 if necessary. Find and mark the centre of the fabric and centre of the chart on pages 46–51. It is recommended that you photocopy the chart parts and tape them together. Note: some colours use more than one skein – see the chart key for details. Mount your fabric in an embroidery frame if you wish.

2 Start stitching from the centre of the chart and work over two linen threads. Use two strands of stranded cotton (floss) for cross stitches but three strands for B5200 cross stitches in the sea and sky. Use one strand to stitch all Kreinik #4 braid cross stitches and backstitches. Using a beading needle and matching thread, attach the beads (see page 97) according to the positions shown on the chart.

3 Once all the stitching is complete, frame the design as a picture (see page 98) or make up as a wall hanging.

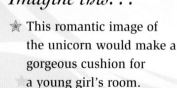

Imagine this...

☆ This romantic image of the unicorn would make a gorgeous cushion for a young girl's room.

☆ This magical creature would transform a ready-made bag into something really special. Stitch on 16-count Aida to make a smaller finished size.

One of the smaller mythical beasts designs charted on page 52 has been used to decorate this little trinket pot. Work on 14-count Aida – a bright colour like this red works well – using two strands of thread for cross stitch and one for backstitch.

. . . through his mane and tail the high wind sings,
Fanning the hairs, who wave like feather'd wings.

(*Venus and Adonis*, William Shakespeare)

Part 1

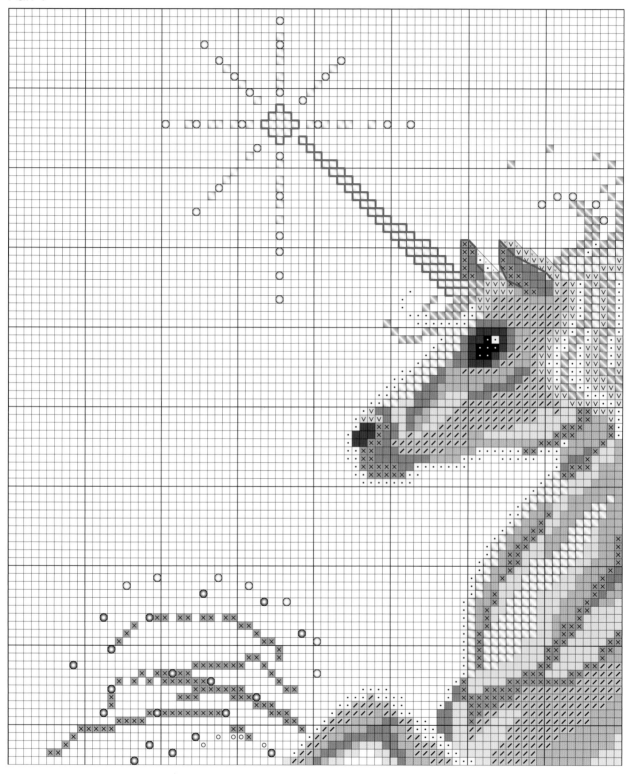

Part 2

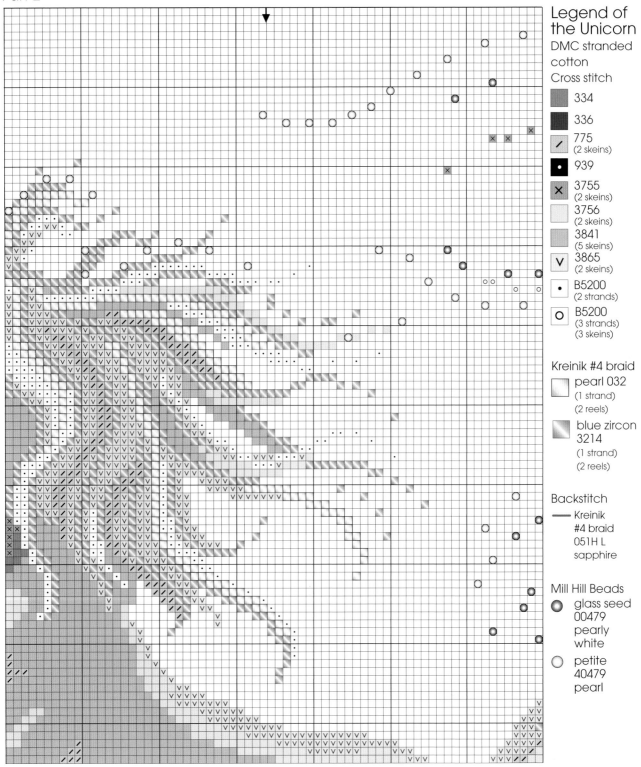

Legend of
the Unicorn

DMC stranded
cotton
Cross stitch

▨	334
▨	336
╱	775 (2 skeins)
▪	939
✕	3755 (2 skeins)
▢	3756 (2 skeins)
▨	3841 (5 skeins)
V	3865 (2 skeins)
•	B5200 (2 strands)
○	B5200 (3 strands) (3 skeins)

Kreinik #4 braid

▨	pearl 032 (1 strand) (2 reels)
▨	blue zircon 3214 (1 strand) (2 reels)

Backstitch

—	Kreinik #4 braid 051H L sapphire

Mill Hill Beads

◉	glass seed 00479 pearly white
○	petite 40479 pearl

Part 3

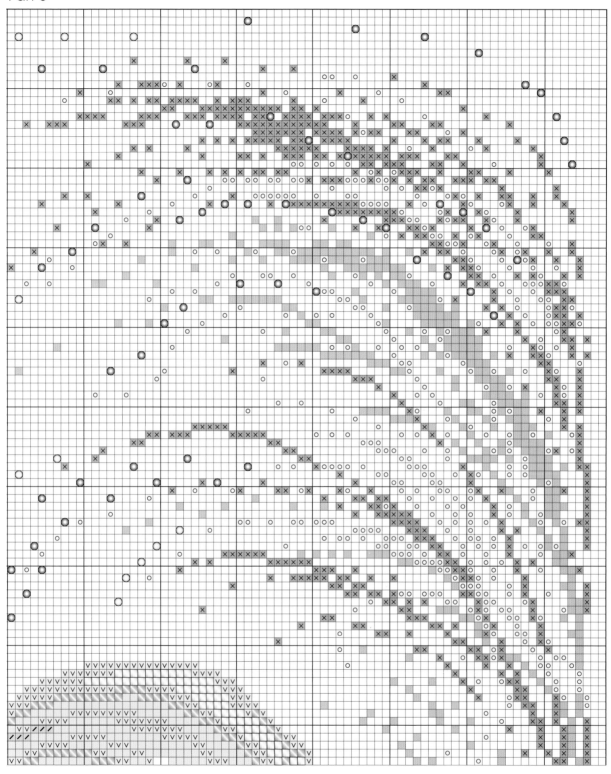

Part 4

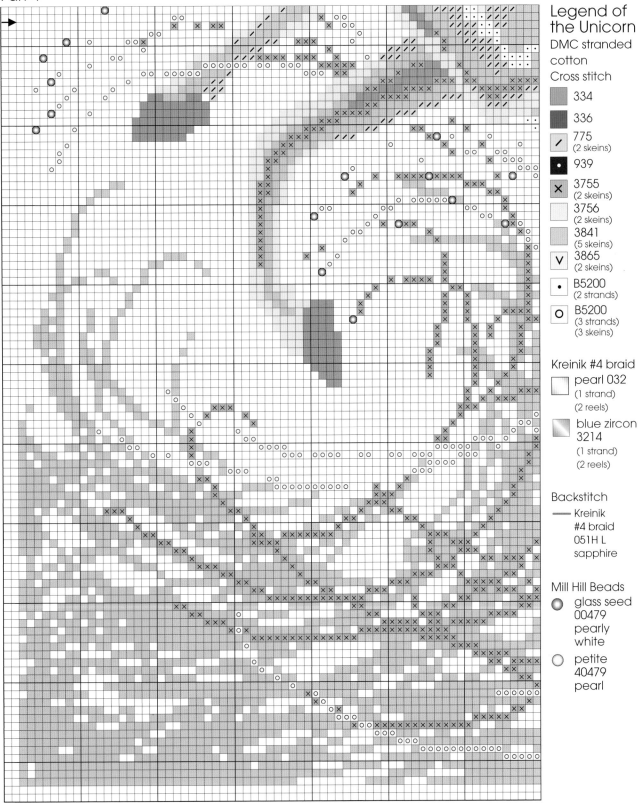

Legend of
the Unicorn
DMC stranded
cotton
Cross stitch

	334
	336
/	775 (2 skeins)
•	939
×	3755 (2 skeins)
	3756 (2 skeins)
	3841 (5 skeins)
V	3865 (2 skeins)
•	B5200 (2 strands)
O	B5200 (3 strands) (3 skeins)

Kreinik #4 braid
pearl 032
(1 strand)
(2 reels)

blue zircon
3214
(1 strand)
(2 reels)

Backstitch
— Kreinik
#4 braid
051H L
sapphire

Mill Hill Beads
⊙ glass seed
00479
pearly
white

○ petite
40479
pearl

Part 5

Part 6

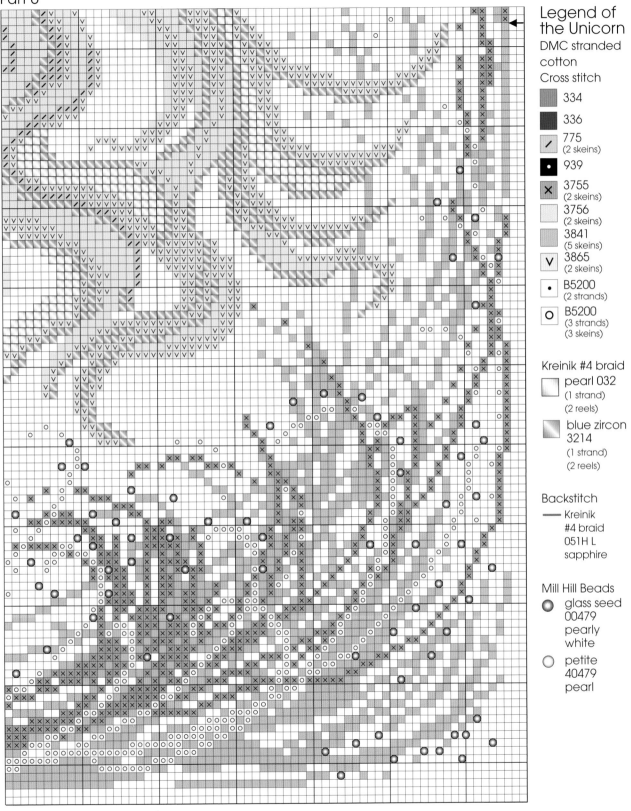

Legend of the Unicorn

DMC stranded cotton

Cross stitch

▓	334
▓	336
╱	775 (2 skeins)
▪	939
✕	3755 (2 skeins)
░	3756 (2 skeins)
▒	3841 (5 skeins)
v	3865 (2 skeins)
•	B5200 (2 strands)
o	B5200 (3 strands) (3 skeins)

Kreinik #4 braid

▢	pearl 032 (1 strand) (2 reels)
◪	blue zircon 3214 (1 strand) (2 reels)

Backstitch

—	Kreinik #4 braid 051H L sapphire

Mill Hill Beads

⬤	glass seed 00479 pearly white
◯	petite 40479 pearl

1 Stitch count: 28h x 29w
Design size: 5 x 5cm (2 x 2in)

2 Stitch count: 41h x 37w
Design size: 7.5 x 7cm (3 x 2¾in)

3 Stitch count: 29h x 36w
Design size: 5 x 6.5cm (2 x 2½in)

4 Stitch count: 30h x 30w
Design size: 5.5 x 5.5cm (2⅛ x 2⅛in)

5 Stitch count: 44h x 30w
Design size: 8 x 5.5cm (3⅛ x 2⅛in)

6 Stitch count: 43h x 39w
Design size: 7.5 x 7cm (3 x 2¾in)

Mythical Beasts

DMC stranded cotton

Cross stitch	Backstitch
■ 310	— 310
▨ E3821 Light Effects	— E3821 Light Effects

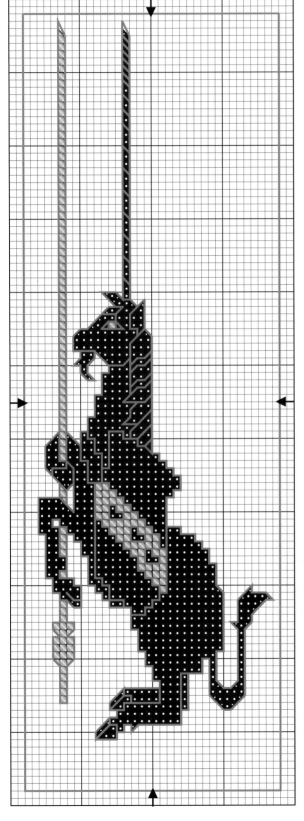

Heraldry Unicorn Stitch count: 106h x 36w
Design size: 19.3 x 6.5cm (7½ x 2½in)

*The unicorn is much used in heraldry and this design has
a deliberately chivalric look. Use the chart here to create a
bookmark and work the design on red 14-count Aida or another
bold fabric colour of your choice. Use two strands of thread for
full and three-quarter cross stitch and one for backstitch. When
the stitching is complete, trim the bookmark to the size you
require and fray the edges for a decorative look.*

Butterfly Fairies

You can chase a butterfly all over the field and never catch it. But if you sit quietly in the grass it will come and sit on your shoulder.

(Author unknown)

A Native American legend says, 'If you have a wish, capture a butterfly and whisper your wish to it. Since butterflies cannot speak your secret is in their safekeeping. Release the butterfly and it will carry your wish to the Great Spirit, who alone knows the thoughts of butterflies.' So, in setting the butterfly free you restore nature's balance and as a reward your wish will be granted.

Butterflies symbolize change and renewed life and are often linked to nature spirits and fey fairy souls. In the fading light of a summer evening it is not difficult to imagine that these lovely creatures are fairy folk fluttering between their favourite flowers, carrying our secret dreams with them. This chapter features six charming fairies and their flowers – perfect for pictures, cards and a range of gifts.

Butterfly Fairy Pictures

The six butterfly fairy designs in this chapter are not only utterly charming but simple to stitch and versatile, and you are sure to find many uses for them – see some suggestions below and opposite. The butterfly bands with each design are a bonus feature, perfect for quick-stitch projects. The designs can be repeated to any length desired.

**You will need
(for each butterfly fairy)**

⭐ 23 x 18cm (9 x 7in)
14-count pale sea green
Aida, (Zweigart code 6150)

⭐ Tapestry needle size 24

⭐ DMC stranded cotton (floss)
as listed in chart key

1 Prepare for work, finding and marking the centre of the fabric and the centre of the relevant chart on pages 58–63. Stitch counts and design sizes are given with the charts. Use an embroidery frame if you wish.

2 Start stitching from the centre of the chart, working over one block of Aida. Use two strands of stranded cotton (floss) for cross stitches and French knots and one strand for backstitches. If working a butterfly band, work from the centre of the band outwards, repeating the pattern as desired.

3 Once all the stitching is complete, make up as desired. For an individual picture see page 98 and for a card see page 100. To make up three designs as a triptych, as shown on the previous page, it is best to take your pieces of work to a framer who can cut a triple-aperture mount accurately.

This White Admiral Fairy is drinking in the scent of her favourite flower, the honeysuckle. The fresh summery colours would be perfect adorning a simple bag. ➡

Imagine this...

⭐ These designs would make delightful individually framed pictures, perhaps framed similarly and hung as a group.

⭐ Three of the designs could be worked as a triptych, as shown on page 55.

⭐ Why not arrange three of the fairies vertically and make up as a bell pull?

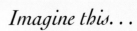

The jaunty Red Admiral Fairy nestling into his favourite poppy flower would make a great decoration on the front of a gardening notebook or journal.

Imagine this. . .

⭐ The six butterfly and flower band designs charted on pages 58–63 are ideal for creating quick greetings cards, with a message of your choice.

⭐ Use the bands to create bookmarks to give as gifts to family and friends.

⭐ Stitch the butterfly bands on Aida or linen bands, repeating the design as necessary to make decorative edgings for table linen or bed linen.

This delicate little Fritillary Fairy amid pink dog roses would make a lovely door sign, perhaps with a child's name cross stitched above the design. ➡

The band designs accompanying each fairy chart are very pretty worked singly, as shown here, or repeated as a decorative border.

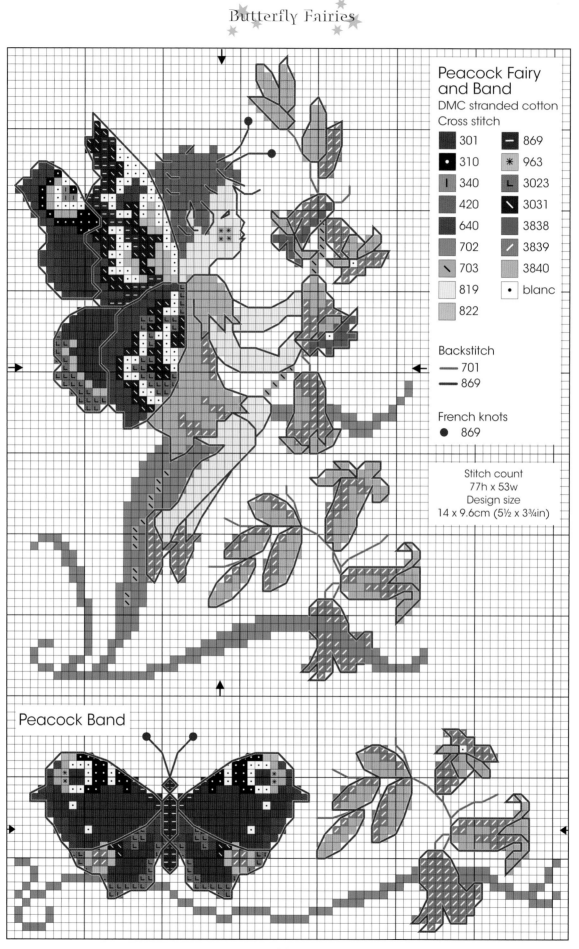

Peacock Fairy and Band

DMC stranded cotton
Cross stitch

▨	301	—	869
▨	310	✳	963
I	340	L	3023
▨	420	╲	3031
▨	640	▨	3838
▨	702	╱	3839
╲	703	▨	3840
▨	819	•	blanc
▨	822		

Backstitch
— 701
— 869

French knots
● 869

Stitch count
77h x 53w
Design size
14 x 9.6cm (5½ x 3¾in)

Peacock Band

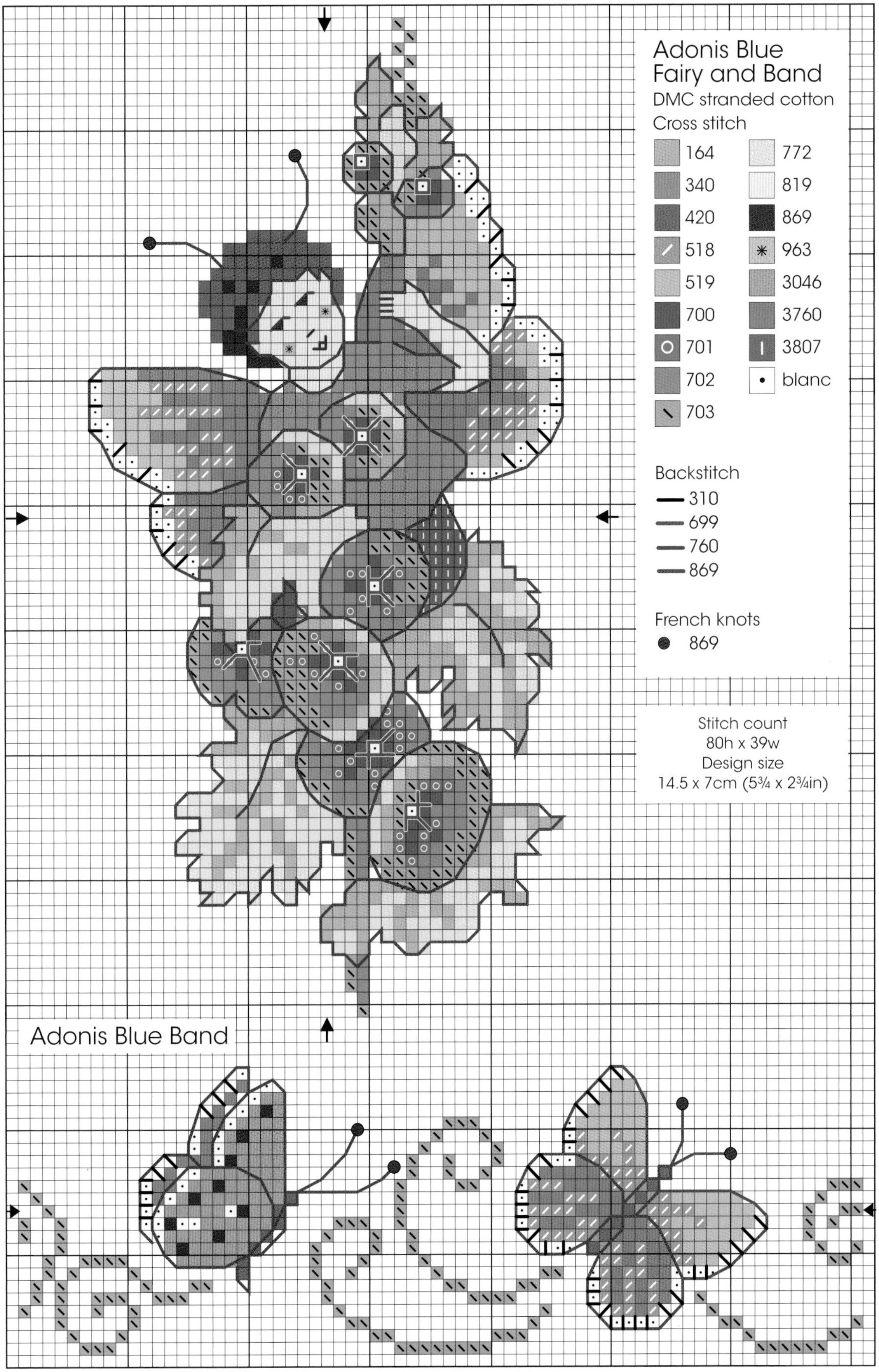

**Adonis Blue
Fairy and Band**
DMC stranded cotton
Cross stitch

164		772
340		819
420		869
518		963
519		3046
700		3760
701		3807
702		blanc
703		

Backstitch
— 310
— 699
— 760
— 869

French knots
● 869

Stitch count
80h x 39w
Design size
14.5 x 7cm (5¾ x 2¾in)

Adonis Blue Band

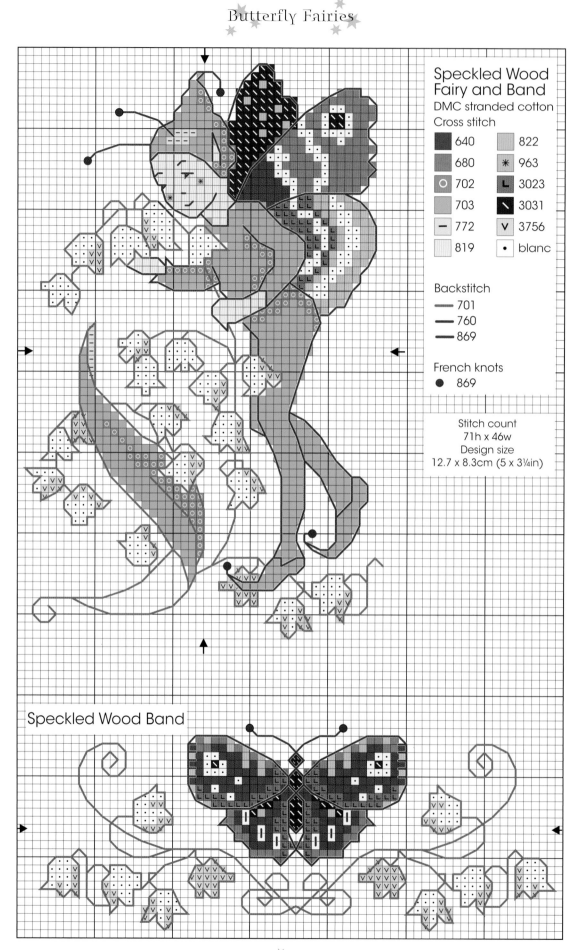

Speckled Wood Fairy and Band

DMC stranded cotton

Cross stitch

■	640		822
■	680	✳	963
O	702	L	3023
	703	╲	3031
–	772	V	3756
	819	•	blanc

Backstitch
— 701
— 760
— 869

French knots
● 869

Stitch count
71h x 46w
Design size
12.7 x 8.3cm (5 x 3¼in)

Speckled Wood Band

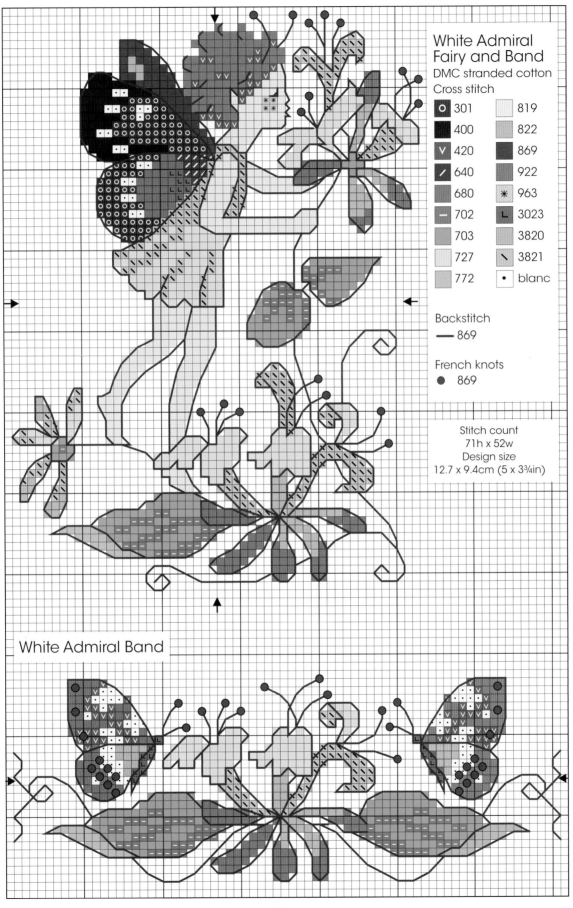

White Admiral
Fairy and Band
DMC stranded cotton
Cross stitch

O	301		819
	400		822
V	420		869
/	640		922
L	680	*	963
−	702	L	3023
	703		3820
	727	\	3821
	772	•	blanc

Backstitch
—— 869

French knots
● 869

Stitch count
71h x 52w
Design size
12.7 x 9.4cm (5 x 3¾in)

White Admiral Band

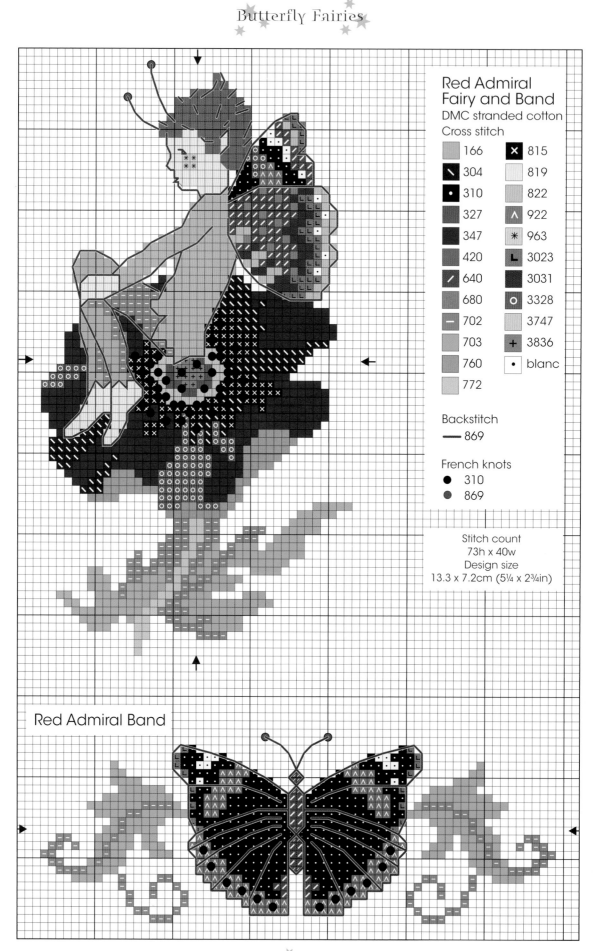

Red Admiral Fairy and Band

DMC stranded cotton

Cross stitch

166		✗	815
304			819
310			822
327		∧	922
347		✳	963
420		L	3023
640			3031
680		○	3328
702			3747
703		+	3836
760		•	blanc
772			

Backstitch
——— 869

French knots
● 310
● 869

Stitch count
73h x 40w
Design size
13.3 x 7.2cm (5¼ x 2¾in)

Red Admiral Band

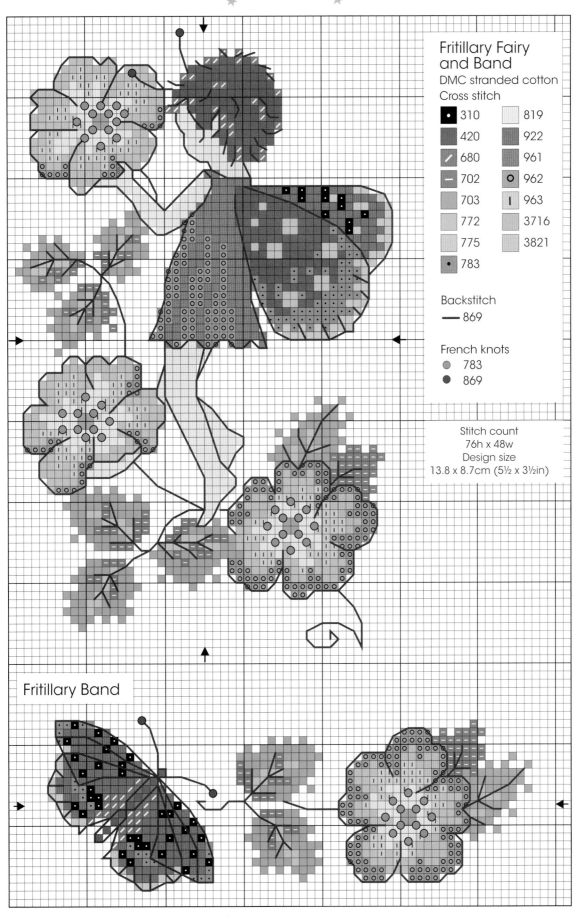

**Fritillary Fairy
and Band**

DMC stranded cotton
Cross stitch

■	310		819
	420		922
/	680		961
–	702	O	962
	703	I	963
	772		3716
	775		3821
•	783		

Backstitch
—— 869

French knots
● 783
● 869

Stitch count
76h x 48w
Design size
13.8 x 8.7cm (5½ x 3½in)

Fritillary Band

Queen of the Night

Our vernal signs the Ram begins,
Then comes the Bull, in May the Twins;
The Crab in June, near Leo shines,
And Virgo ends the northern signs.

(E. Cobham Brewer, 1898)

The Queen of the Night is an enigmatic figure in a world of mystery and fantasy. Her image possibly came from Greek mythology as Hecate, a powerful goddess who had three aspects – goddess of fertility, goddess of the moon and Queen of the Night. I've used this mythical figure to create this stunning design, taking her connection with the moon and the night and arranging her within the astrological signs of the zodiac.

The word 'zodiac' comes from the Greek, meaning 'circle of little animals' and centuries ago the Greeks divided the heavens into twelve segments, through which the sun and planets were seen to move against the stars. The Greeks linked the main stars in these segments or constellations to create identifiable human and animal shapes – such as a crab, bull, scorpion and lion.

These motifs are still popular today and I've displayed them watched over by the mystical Queen of the Night. The design is stitched on a deep blue Aida, to echo the night sky. Stitch the whole design, with its glittering motifs, or work individual parts for small gifts and keepsakes.

Zodiac Picture

The twelve signs of the zodiac encircle the beautiful Queen of the Night. Each zodiac motif is accompanied by its symbol and both can be stitched separately as cards or gift tags. See page 71 for the zodiac dates. Instead of framing the design it would make a beautiful circular cushion.

Stitch count
210h x 212w

Design size
38 x 38cm (15 x 15in)

You will need

✫ 51 x 51cm (24 x 24in) 14-count deep blue Aida (Zweigart code 567)

✫ Tapestry needle size 24 and a beading needle

✫ DMC stranded cottons (floss) as listed in the chart key

✫ Kreinik #4 Very Fine Braid as listed in chart key

✫ Mill Hill glass seed beads 03048 red

1 Prepare for work, referring to page 95 if necessary. Find and mark the centre of the fabric and centre of the chart on pages 68–71. For your own use you could photocopy the chart parts and tape them together. Note: some colours use more than one skein or reel – see chart key for details. Mount your fabric in an embroidery frame if you wish.

2 Start stitching from the centre of the chart and the centre of the fabric working over one block of Aida. Use two strands of stranded cotton (floss) for full and three-quarter stitches and one strand for backstitches. Use one strand for Kreinik #4 braid cross stitches. With a beading needle and matching thread, attach the beads (see page 97) according to the positions on the chart.

3 Once all the stitching is complete, frame the design as a picture (see page 98).

The Zodiac motifs from the main chart can be stitched and made up into smaller projects and would be perfect for birthday cards as these two pictures show. Stitch the designs on white 14-count Aida or a colour of your choice and use two strands of thread for cross stitch and one for backstitch. Add embellishments of your choice. See page 100 for mounting work in cards.

The Balance brings autumnal fruits,
The Scorpion stings, the Archer shoots;
December's Goat brings wintry blast,
Aquarius rain, the fish come last.

(E. Cobham Brewer, 1898)

Top left

Queen of the Night

DMC stranded cotton
Cross stitch

— 301	↑ 435	S 729	I 807	/ 948		3766 (7 skeins)		3832	
• 310 (3 skeins)		436	\ 742	T 918	⌐ 3072		3770	/ 3853
Z 400	U 437	− 747	919		3756	\ 3778	< 3854
	413		676		754	L 920	V 3761	∧ 3823	• 3865
+ 434	C 677	× 758		921		3765	■ 3829	

Kreinik #4 Braid
Cross stitch (one strand)

006HL blue (2 reels)	
012 purple (2 reels)	
019 pewter (3 reels)	
I 101 platinum (3 reels)	

Backstitch
— 801

Mill Hill Seed Beads
● 03048 red

Top right

Bottom left

Queen of the Night

DMC stranded cotton
Cross stitch

− 301	↑ 435	S 729	I 807	/ 948	3766 (7 skeins)	3832
• 310 (3 skeins)	436	\ 742	T 918	⌐ 3072	3770	/ 3853
Z 400	U 437	− 747	919	3756	\ 3778	< 3854
413	676	754	L 920	V 3761	∧ 3823	• 3865
+ 434	C 677	X 758	921	3765	3829	

Kreinik #4 Braid
Cross stitch (one strand)

006HL blue (2 reels)	
012 purple (2 reels)	
019 pewter (3 reels)	
I 101 platinum (3 reels)	

Backstitch
— 801

Mill Hill Seed Beads
⬤ 03048 red

Bottom right

The Zodiac

Aquarius	Jan 20 – Feb 18	Leo	July 21 – Aug 21
Pisces	Feb 20 – Mar 20	Virgo	Aug 22 – Sept 22
Aries	Mar 21 – April 20	Libra	Sept 23 – Oct 22
Taurus	April 21 – May 20	Scorpio	Oct 23 – Nov 22
Gemini	May 21 – June 20	Sagittarius	Nov 23 – Dec 20
Cancer	June 21 – July 20	Capricorn	Dec 21 – Jan 19

Medieval Myths

There drew he forth the brand Excalibur,
And o'er him, drawing it, the winter moon,
Brightening the skirts of a long cloud, ran forth
And sparkled keen with frost against the hilt:

(from 'Morte d'Arthur', Alfred Lord Tennyson)

The inspiration for this chapter came from the architectural style of the medieval period and in particular gargoyles, the grotesque shapes of animals or humans that project from buildings. The term gargoyle comes from the Latin 'gurgulio' and the French 'gargouille', not only meaning 'throat' but also describing the gurgling sound made by water as it ran through the figure.

I wanted to include other iconic motifs from the worlds of fantasy and mythology and use them to create an alphabet with a distinctly Gothic look. The Green Man is an ancient figure in mythology and represents nature. The image of the gryphon (or griffin) – half lion, half eagle – is an enduring one and in heraldry represents strength and vigilance. The owl has dual symbolism of wisdom and darkness, while the dragon represents prosperity and a benevolent force.

The letters of the alphabet, stitched in gold metallic thread, can be used on their own to decorate cards and small gifts, while the combined letters make an impressive design for a notebook or a name picture, as seen opposite.

Gothic Alphabet

Each letter of this bold alphabet can be stitched individually or a group of motifs combined to make up words or names. The letters are shown here stitched on red Aida but many other colours would be suitable. See page 82 for another, more feminine alphabet.

Stitch count
Various, 50h x 51w max

Design size
Various, 9 x 9cm
(3½ x 3½in) max

You will need (for one letter)

☆ 15 x 15cm (6 x 6in) 14-count red Aida (Zweigart code 954)

☆ Tapestry needle size 24

☆ Kreinik #4 Very Fine Braid as listed in chart key

To stitch a single letter

1 Prepare for work and find and mark the centre of the letter to be stitched. Start stitching from the centre of the letter and the centre of the fabric, working over one block of Aida and using one strand of Kreinik thread for cross stitch and backstitch.

2 Once all the stitching is complete, make up into a card (see page 100) or small items and gifts (see page 81).

To stitch a name

1 Choose the name or word you wish to stitch and ensure you have sufficient fabric to stitch it on. The letters are a maximum of 50 stitches tall, so stitched on 14-count fabric this would produce a finished height of 9cm (3½in), plus additional fabric for making up. To work out the overall width of the name, count the number of stitches across each letter (using the charted letters). Add these together and add another two Aida squares between each letter. Divide this total number of stitches by the stitch count of the fabric to show the finished width of the stitching. Add sufficient fabric for making up. (See also Calculating Design Size on page 95.)

2 When you are sure the name will fit on the piece of fabric you are using, stitch the letters as described above. Finish the project by framing or making up in another way of your choice – see pages 77 and 79 for ideas.

Gothic Alphabet

Kreinik #4 Braid

Cross stitch   Backstitch
(one strand)   (one strand)

███ 028 citron   ── 005 black

The letters have slightly different stitch counts.
The name example shown opposite allows
two squares between letters.

Gothic Alphabet
Kreinik #4 Braid

Cross stitch | Backstitch
(one strand) | (one strand)

☒ 028 citron   — 005 black

The letters have slightly different stitch counts.
The name example shown on page 74 allows
two squares between letters.

Imagine this . . .

⭐ Use the alphabet to stitch a name and make up as a door sign. The finished embroidery can be wrapped over a piece of thick card and secured with craft glue, with a ribbon loop added to hang the sign.

⭐ You could also stitch a name for a diary, fraying the edges of the finished embroidery and using double-sided tape to fix it to the front of the book.

Gothic Alphabet
Kreinik #4 Braid

Cross stitch	Backstitch
(one strand)	(one strand)

▨ 028 citron   — 005 black

The letters have slightly different stitch counts. The name example shown on page 74 allows two squares between letters.

Imagine this...

☆ Companies such as Charles Craft and Framecraft (see Suppliers) have a wide
range of items for embroidery. One of the letters would look very attractive in
a crystal or wooden trinket pot and make a lovely gift.

☆ Experiment with the alphabet by changing the colour of the fabric and
threads for a different look. For example, a black fabric could be used, with
the letters changed to silver and the backstitches to red. Experiment with
variegated threads too.

Gothic Alphabet
Kreinik #4 Braid

Cross stitch	Backstitch
(one strand)	(one strand)

028 citron   —— 005 black

The letters have slightly different stitch counts.
The name example shown on page 74 allows
two squares between letters.

There are many items made for embroidery, such as coasters and paperweights, which would be perfect to display a single letter. The letter T has been stitched and mounted into a paperweight (below), while the letter E adorns a coaster (left). You could also stitch an initial for a key ring.

Scroll Alphabet

This alphabet is also in a Gothic style but is more feminine and delicate, with fine scrolling patterns in silver thread stitched in backstitch around the letters. The letters would look very pretty stitched up for cards and small gifts. The name Marie is shown below – see page 74 for instructions on stitching a name.

Stitch count
18h x 28w max

Design size
3.2 x 5cm (1 ¼ x 2in) max

You will need (for one letter)

☆ 15 x 15cm (6 x 6in) 14-count black Aida (or other colour of your choice)

☆ Tapestry needle size 24

☆ DMC stranded cotton (floss) and Light Effects thread as listed in chart key

1 To stitch a single letter, prepare your fabric for work and find and mark the centre of the charted letter. Start stitching from the centre of the letter and centre of the fabric working over one block of Aida, using two strands of thread for cross stitch and one strand for backstitch.

2 Once all the stitching is complete, make up into individual cards or use to decorate small gifts.

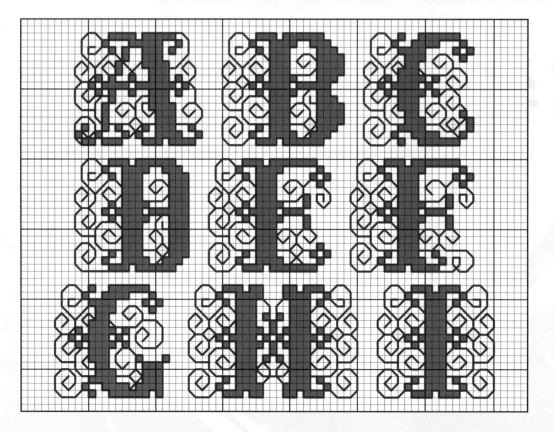

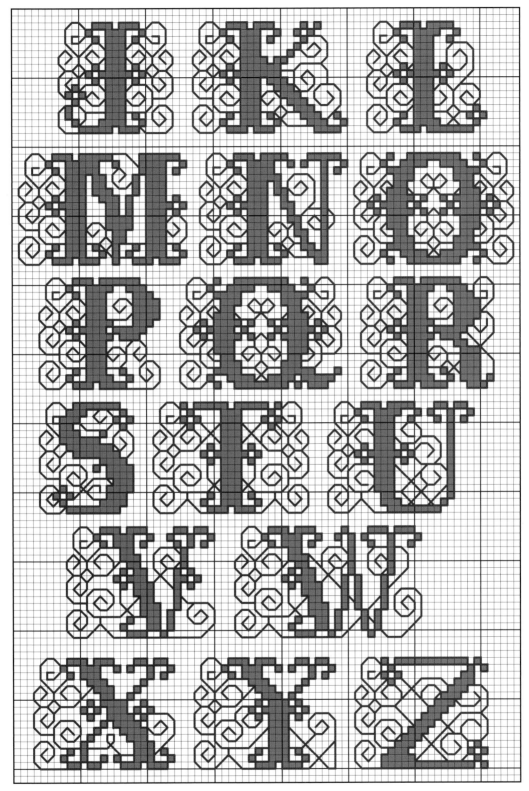

Scroll Alphabet

DMC stranded cotton

Cross stitch   Backstitch

⬛ 3746   —— E168
                    Light Effects

Each letter is 18 stitches high. The width of the letters varies between 16 and 28 stitches. The name example shown opposite allows one square between letters.

Power of the Dragon

Who entereth herein, a conqueror hath bin;
Who slayeth the dragon, the shield he shall win.

(from *The Fall of the House of Usher*, Edgar Allen Poe)

East to west, north to south, in the heavens and in the underworld, there is a dragon for every age and every culture and these magical creatures continue to fascinate us today. The Anglo-Saxon word 'draken' is probably a Greek derivative, either from 'draco' meaning dragon or large snake, or from the verb 'derkein', which means to see clearly. Dragons were credited with clear sight, wisdom and the ability to foretell the future.

For centuries the Chinese people have loved, revered and respected dragons for their awesome wisdom and power. In medieval Britain and Europe, however, dragons were given a more negative image and Christian heroes were often depicted as knights in shining armour who slew a dragon after a fierce battle – symbolically the triumph of good over evil.

My dragon is more likely to protect than to devour. I choose to stitch him on a red background with the addition of gold metallic thread and green beads to create the most striking image. The design makes a fantastic picture and would also be wonderful as a wall hanging.

Dragon Picture

This magnificent creature is predominantly stitched in shades of green and gold, so choosing a red Aida created maximum contrast. Backstitched in black the design makes a bold statement. I've also charted some smaller dragon designs on pages 92–93, and two of these have been made up into a card (below) and a small wall hanging (page 93).

Stitch count
243h x 163w

Design size
44.3 x 29.5cm
(17½ x 11¾ in)

You will need
- ☆ 71 x 56cm (28 x 22in) 14-count red Aida (Zweigart code 954)
- ☆ Tapestry needle size 24 and a beading needle
- ☆ DMC stranded cottons (floss) as listed in the key
- ☆ Kreinik #4 Very Fine Braid 017HL white gold (or DMC Light Effects E677)
- ☆ Mill Hill seed beads 02054 green
- ☆ Suitable picture frame

1 Prepare for work, referring to page 95 if necessary. Find and mark the centre of the fabric and centre of the chart on pages 88–91. For your own use you could photocopy the four chart parts and tape them together. Note: some colours use more than one skein – see chart key for details. Mount your fabric in an embroidery frame if you wish.

2 Start stitching from the centre of the chart working over one block of Aida. Use two strands of stranded cotton (floss) for full and three-quarter cross stitches and one strand for backstitches. Use one strand for all Kreinik #4 braid cross stitches. Attach the beads where indicated on the chart, using a beading needle and matching thread (see page 97).

3 Once all the stitching is complete, frame the design as a picture (see page 98).

This colourful card would be perfect for a birthday or perhaps for Father's Day. It was stitched on antique white 14-count Aida using two strands of thread for cross stitch and one for backstitch and mounted into a ready-made double-fold card (see page 100). The embellishments used are from a sheet of stick-ons with an oriental theme.

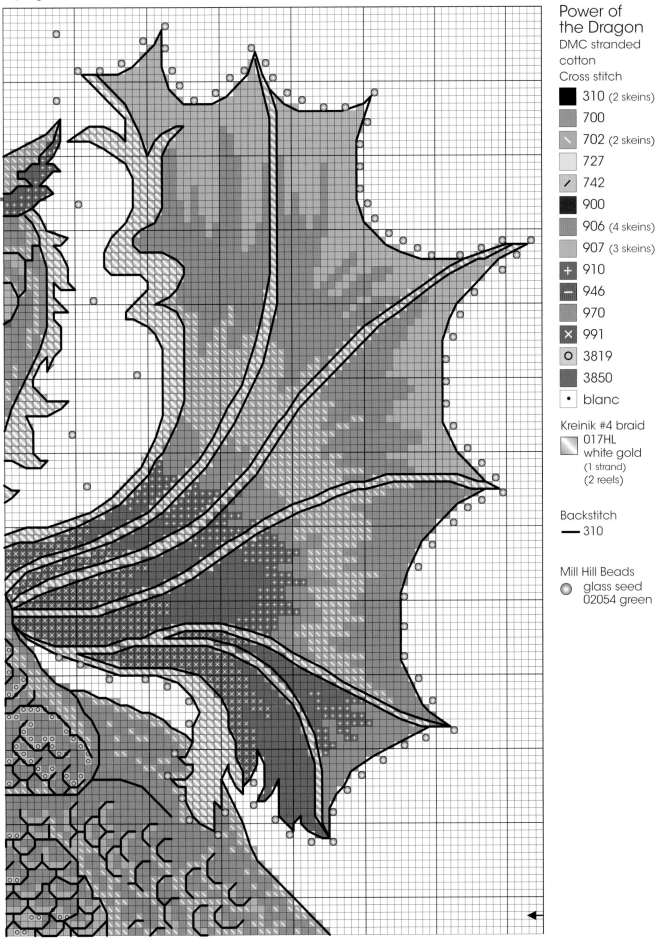

Power of
the Dragon
DMC stranded
cotton
Cross stitch

■ 310 (2 skeins)
▨ 700
◣ 702 (2 skeins)
▨ 727
╱ 742
▨ 900
▨ 906 (4 skeins)
▨ 907 (3 skeins)
+ 910
− 946
▨ 970
✕ 991
○ 3819
▨ 3850
• blanc

Kreinik #4 braid
▨ 017HL
white gold
(1 strand)
(2 reels)

Backstitch
— 310

Mill Hill Beads
◉ glass seed
02054 green

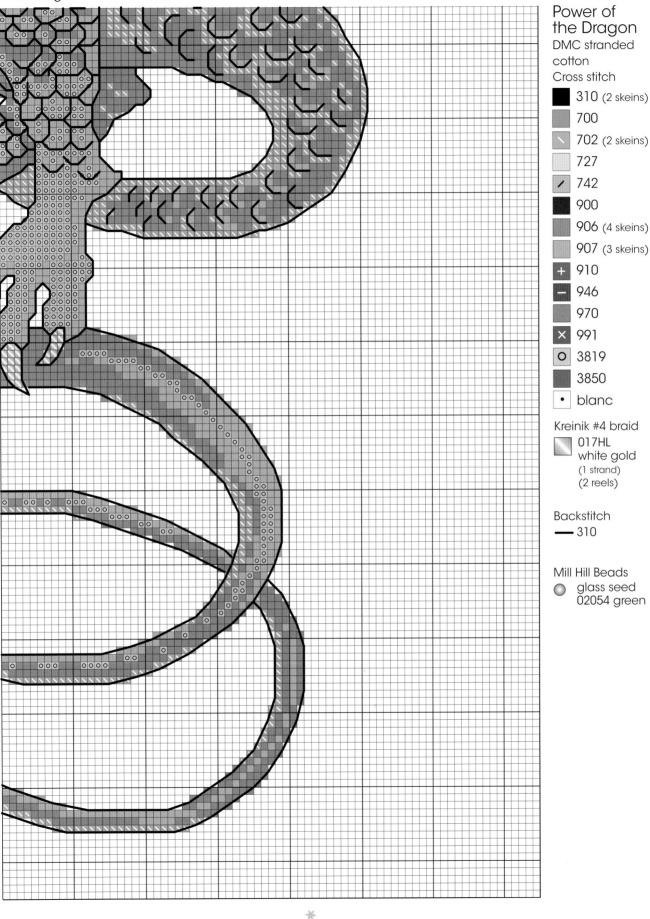

Power of the Dragon

DMC stranded cotton
Cross stitch

■	310 (2 skeins)
	700
◣	702 (2 skeins)
	727
◿	742
■	900
	906 (4 skeins)
	907 (3 skeins)
+	910
–	946
	970
×	991
O	3819
	3850
•	blanc

Kreinik #4 braid

◤	017HL white gold (1 strand) (2 reels)

Backstitch
—— 310

Mill Hill Beads
⊙ glass seed 02054 green

Tall dragon   Stitch count: 52h x 44w
Design size: 9.5 x 8cm (3¾ x 3⅛in)

Small dragon   Stitch count: 36h x 32w
Design size: 6.5 x 5.8cm (2½ x 2¼in)

Long dragon   Stitch count: 44h x 83w
Design size: 8 x 15cm (3⅛ x 6in)

Red dragons   Stitch count: 44h x 12w
Design size: 8 x 2.1cm (3⅛ x ⅝in)

Dragon Motifs
DMC stranded cotton
Cross stitch

			Backstitch
● 310	╱ 742	○ 3819	— 310
700	900	3850	
702	906	• blanc	
727	907	E168 Light Effects	

92

Chinese dragon   Stitch count: 100h x 35w
Design size: 18 x 6.3cm (7 x 2½in)

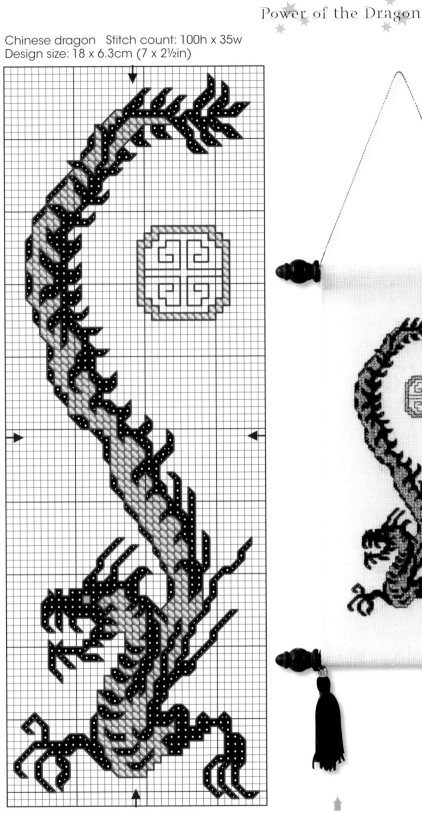

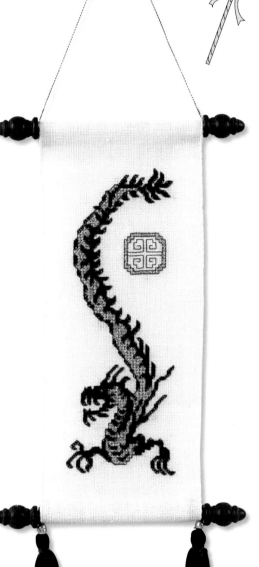

Imagine this...

★ The dragon designs on these pages are satisfyingly quick to stitch and can be used for a range of greetings cards – from birthdays to Chinese New Year celebrations. With the limited colour range it would be easy to change the colours used, perhaps from green and silver-gilt to blue and bronze.

★ The designs would also make great little wall hangings or bell pulls – as the picture, left, shows.

★ The two green dragons (far left, top) are just the right shape to be stitched and mounted into a box lid. A wooden box in a rich mahogany colour would complement the designs well.

Chinese Dragon
DMC stranded cotton
Cross stitch   Backstitch

■ 310   —— 900

▨ 702

▨ E168

This dramatic little bell pull features a smaller dragon. The design was stitched over two threads of antique white 28-count linen band using two strands of thread for cross stitch and one for backstitch. Two black tassels embellish the project beautifully. See page 102 for making up the bell pull.

Materials, Techniques and Stitches

This section is useful to beginners as it describes the materials and equipment required and the basic techniques and stitches needed to work the projects. Refer to page 98 for making up methods and see Suppliers on page 104 for useful addresses.

Materials

Very few materials are required for cross stitch embroidery, although some of the projects in this book have been given an additional sparkle and texture by the use of seed beads.

Fabrics

The designs have mostly been worked on a blockweave embroidery fabric called Aida. If you change the gauge (count) of the material, that is the number of holes per inch, then the size of the finished work will alter accordingly. Some of the designs have been stitched on linen evenweave and in this case need to be worked over two fabric threads instead of one block.

Threads

The projects have been stitched with DMC stranded embroidery cotton (floss) but you could match the colours to other thread ranges – ask at your local needlework store. The six-stranded skeins can easily be split into separate threads. The project instructions tell you how many strands to use. Some projects use one strand of a Kreinik metallic thread for added glitter. Some of the larger designs use more than one skein or reel of thread and this information is contained in the chart key.

Needles

Tapestry needles, available in different sizes, are used for cross stitch as they have a rounded point and therefore do not snag the fabric. A thinner, beading needle will be needed to attach seed beads.

Frames

It is a matter of personal preference as to whether you use an embroidery frame or hoop to keep your fabric taut while stitching. Generally speaking, working with a frame helps to keep the tension even and prevent distortion, while working without a frame is faster and less cumbersome. There are various types on the market – look in your local needlework store.

Techniques

Cross stitch embroidery requires few techniques but your stitching will look its best if you follow these simple guidelines.

Preparing the Fabric

Before starting work, check the design size given with each project and make sure that this is the size you require for your finished embroidery. Your fabric should be at least 5cm (2in) larger all the way round than the finished size of the stitching, to allow for making up. Before beginning to stitch, neaten the fabric edges either by hemming or zigzagging to prevent fraying as you work.

Finding the Fabric Centre

Marking the centre of the fabric is important, regardless of which direction you work from, in order to stitch the design centrally on the fabric. To find the centre, fold the fabric in half horizontally and then vertically and tack (baste) along the folds (or use tailor's chalk). The centre point is where the two lines of tacking meet. This point on the fabric should correspond to the centre of the chart. Remove these lines on completion of the work.

Calculating Design Size

Each project gives the stitch count and finished design size but if you want to work the design on a different count fabric you will need to re-calculate the finished size. Divide the numbers of stitches in the design by the fabric count number, e.g., 140 x 140 ÷ 14-count = a design size of 10 x 10in (25.5 x 25.5cm). Working on evenweave means working over two threads, so divide the fabric count by two before you start calculating.

Starting and Finishing Stitching

Avoid using knots when starting and finishing as this will make your work lumpy when mounted. Instead, bring the needle up at the start of the first stitch, leaving a 'tail' of about 2.5cm (1in) at the back. Secure the tail by working the first few stitches over it and then cut off the knot. Start new threads by first passing the needle through several stitches on the back of the work.

To finish off thread, pass the needle through some nearby stitches on the back of the work, then cut the thread off close to the fabric.

Washing and Pressing

If you need to wash your finished embroidery, first make sure the stranded cottons are colourfast by washing them in tepid water and mild soap. Rinse well and lay out flat to dry completely before stitching. Wash completed embroideries in the same way. Iron on a medium setting, covering the ironing board with a thick layer of towelling. Place stitching right side down and press gently.

Using Charts and Keys

The charts in this book are easy to work from. Each square on the chart represents one stitch. Each coloured square, or coloured square with a symbol, represents a thread colour, with the code number given in the chart key. A few of the designs use fractional stitches (three-quarter cross stitches) to give more definition to the design. Solid coloured lines show where backstitches or long stitches are to be worked. French knots are shown by coloured circles. Larger coloured circles indicate beads.

Each complete chart has arrows at the side to show the centre point, which you could mark with a pen. Where the charts have been split over several pages, the key is repeated. For your own use, you could colour photocopy and enlarge charts, taping the parts together.

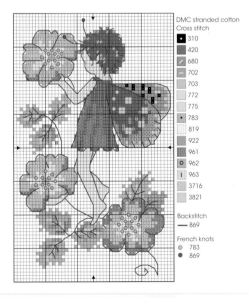

DMC stranded cotton
Cross stitch
- 310
- 420
- 680
- 702
- 703
- 772
- 775
- 783
- 819
- 922
- 961
- 962
- 963
- 3716
- 3821

Backstitch
— 869

French knots
- 783
- 869

The Stitches

The stitches used for the projects in this book are all extremely easy to work – follow the instructions and diagrams here.

Backstitch

Backstitches are used to give definition to parts of a design and to outline areas. In some designs the backstitch doesn't follow the cross stitch exactly but uses a more 'sketchy' style. Follow Fig 1, bringing the needle up at 1 and down at 2. Then bring the needle up again at 3, and so on.

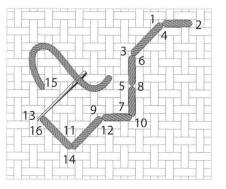

Fig 1 Working backstitch

Cross Stitch

A cross stitch can be worked singly over one block of Aida (Fig 2a) or over two threads of linen or evenweave fabric (Fig 2b). You can also work cross stitch in two journeys, working a number of half stitches in a line and completing the stitches on the return journey (Fig 2c).

To make a cross stitch over one block of Aida, bring the needle up through the fabric at the bottom left side of the stitch (number 1 on Fig 2a) and cross diagonally to the top right corner (2). Push the needle through the hole and bring up through the bottom right corner (3), crossing the fabric diagonally to the top left corner to finish the stitch (4). To work the next stitch, come up through the bottom right corner of the first stitch and repeat the sequence above.

To work a line of cross stitches, stitch the first part of the stitch as above and repeat these half cross stitches along the row. Complete the crosses on the way back. Note: for neat work, always finish the cross stitch with the top stitches lying in the same diagonal direction.

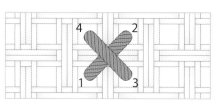

Fig 2a Working a single cross stitch on Aida fabric

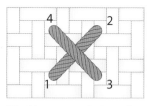

Fig 2b Working cross stitch on linen or evenweave fabric

Fig 2c Working cross stitch in two journeys

French Knot

French knots have been used as highlights and details in some of the designs, in various colours. To work, follow Fig 3, bringing the needle and thread up through the fabric at the exact place where the knot is to be positioned. Wrap the thread once or twice around the needle (depending on how big you like your knots), holding the thread firmly close to the needle, then twist the needle back through the fabric as close as possible to where it first emerged. Holding the knot down carefully, pull the thread through to the back leaving the knot on the surface, securing it with one small stitch on the back.

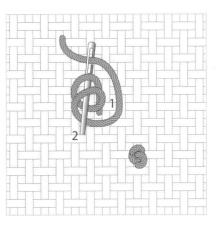

Fig 3 Working a French knot

Long Stitch

You may use this stitch occasionally, for example for flower stamens or butterfly antennae. Simply work a long, straight stitch (Fig 4) starting and finishing at the points indicated on the chart.

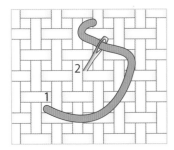

Fig 4 Working a long stitch

Three-quarter Cross Stitch

Three-quarter cross stitches give more detail to a design and can create the illusion of curves. They are shown by a triangle within a square on the charts. Working three-quarter cross stitches is easier on evenweave fabric than Aida (see Fig 5). To work on Aida, work a half stitch across the diagonal and then make a quarter stitch from the other corner into the centre of the Aida square, piercing the fabric and anchoring the half stitch.

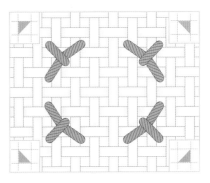

Fig 5 Working three-quarter cross stitch

Attaching Beads

Beads can bring sparkle and texture to your cross stitch embroidery and are a lovely addition to many of the designs in this book. Attach seed beads using ordinary sewing thread that matches the fabric colour and a beading needle or very fine 'sharp' needle and a half or whole cross stitch (Fig 6).

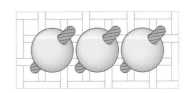

Fig 6 Attaching beads

For some parts of a design, long stitch can be used instead of backstitch

Making Up

The embroideries in this book have been made up in various ways, including pictures, cards, drawstring bags, bell pulls and book marks. The methods used are described here, but the designs are very versatile so why not experiment with other ways? A list of suppliers is given on page 104, most of which will supply a catalogue on request. Metric and imperial measurements have been provided throughout the book but remember to use either one or the other as they are not exactly interchangeable.

Framing as a Picture

There are many stunning pictures in the book and how an embroidery is mounted and framed can make a great deal of difference to the finished look. It is advisable to take your work to a professional framer for a wide choice of mounts and frames, especially if framing as a triptych, as the Butterfly Fairies on page 55.

You will need

★ Piece of plywood or heavyweight card slightly smaller than the frame

★ Suitable picture frame (aperture size to fit embroidery)

★ Adhesive tape or a staple gun

1 Iron your embroidery and trim the edges if necessary. Centre the embroidery on the plywood or card.

2 Fold the edges of the embroidery to the back and use adhesive tape or a staple gun to fix in place.

3 Insert the picture into the frame and secure with adhesive tape or staples.

Mounting Work into Ready-made Items

There are many pre-finished items that are produced to display cross stitch embroidery such as the paperweight and coaster shown here. There are also trays, fire screens, mugs, boxes, mirrors, trinket pots and much more.

To mount work in these products, you generally only need to follow the manufacturer's instructions, but it helps to back the embroidered work using iron-on interfacing – see right.

Using Iron-On Interfacing

Cross stitch embroidery can be stabilized with iron-on interfacing, which also helps prevent fraying if you need to cut the fabric into shape. Double-sided interfacing can be used to fuse your embroidery to another fabric. Interfacing is available from needle-work shops and craft stores.

1 Cut a piece of interfacing a little larger than the finished design size (including any unworked fabric needed to fill an aperture or ready-made item).

2 Set the iron to the manufacturer's recommended heating (usually a medium setting). Do a test first on waste fabric and interfacing to make sure that they will bond without scorching the design.

3 Place the stitching face down on a towel and iron on the interfacing. Trim off any excess fabric.

Attaching Embroidery to a Background Fabric

Attaching an embroidery to a background fabric allows you to make up the embroidery in a more interesting way, in effect framing it with fabric. This is particularly effective when making up a wall hanging.

You will need

✫ Background fabric

✫ Iron-on interfacing, such as Vilene

✫ Decorative braid, tassel and buttons

1 When the embroidery is completed, use the weave of the fabric as a guide to trim to within ten rows of the design. Press the stitched piece and iron the interfacing on the back of the embroidery to stabilize it. Fold over the edges to leave two fabric rows showing around the design. Press these folds into place.

2 Find the centre of the background fabric and the centre of the embroidery, and pin or tack (baste) guidelines for the position of the embroidery. Place the embroidery on the fabric and slipstitch in place with matching thread.

3 Add decorative cord all around the edge of the embroidery, starting at bottom centre and slipstitching it into place. To finish off, you could add a decorative bead or button where the cord ends meet. The top of the fabric could then be folded to the back to make a channel for dowelling to create a wall hanging.

Mounting Work into Cards

Many of the designs or parts of larger designs can be stitched and made up into cards and there are many styles of card mounts available today. Some are simple single-fold cards, while others are pre-folded with three sections, the middle one having a window or aperture for your embroidery.

Mounting Work in a Double-Fold Card

1 To mount embroidery in a ready-made card, position it in the aperture – it should be slightly larger than the aperture, so trim if necessary.

2 Place strips of double-sided adhesive tape on the card to secure the embroidery (some cards already have this in place).

3 Peel the backing from the tape and fold over the third of the card to cover. This can also be secured with tape for a neater finish. For a personal touch add ribbons, bows, buttons, stick-ons and so on to embellish the card.

Mounting Work on a Single-Fold Card

1 To stabilize and stiffen your finished stitching, back it with iron-on interfacing as described on the previous page. Check the embroidery size against the front of the card and trim it to the size required leaving two or three extra rows all round the stitching.

2 Attach the embroidery to the front of your card using double-sided tape or fast-tack craft glue. If desired you could glue decorative cord or thin ribbon around the edges of the embroidery.

If you want a fringed edge, fuse a slightly smaller piece of interfacing to the back of the stitching, allowing some unfused rows or threads all round, which can then be pulled away to form a fringe.

Making a Double-Fold Card

You can make your own double-fold cards easily and this will allow you to choose a card colour to match your embroidery. The instructions below are for a small card but you can change the dimensions by working with a larger piece of cardstock. Choose a weight of card thick enough to support your stitching.

You will need

☆ Thick cardstock in a colour of your choice

☆ Cutting mat

☆ Craft knife and metal ruler

☆ Embossing tool and bone folder (optional)

1 Choose a card colour to complement your embroidery and cut a piece 30 x 12.7cm (12 x 5in) as shown in Fig 7 (or to the size of your choice). On the wrong side of the card, use a pencil to draw two lines dividing the card into three sections of 10cm (4in). Score gently along each line with the back of a craft knife or an embossing tool to make folding easier. Be careful not to cut through the card.

2 In the centre section, mark an aperture slightly bigger than the finished size of the design, leaving a border of about 2.5cm (1in) at the top and bottom and about 1.25cm (½in) at the sides. Place the card on a cutting mat and cut out the aperture with a sharp craft knife and metal ruler, carefully cutting into the corners neatly.

3 Trim the left edge of the first section by 2mm (⅛in) so that it lies flat when folded over to the inside of the card. This will cover the back of the stitching. Fold the left and then the right section on the scored lines – a bone folder will help you to create a nice, sharp fold. The card is now ready for you to mount your embroidery.

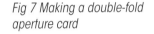

Fig 7 Making a double-fold aperture card

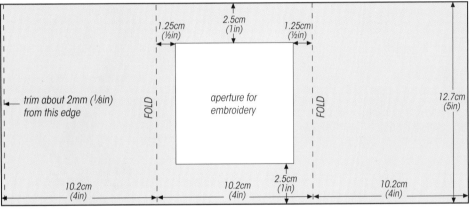

Making a Twisted Cord

A twisted cord can create a decorative edging to your stitching, be placed in the fold of a card or be a tie for gift tags. There are decorative cords available but it is easy to make your own. Choose shades that tone with the embroidery for a co-ordinated look or pick a contrasting colour. Experiment with metallic or other specialist threads for a sumptuous effect.

1 To make a single-colour cord, choose a shade from your embroidery design and cut a length of stranded cotton (floss) about three times longer than the finished cord.

2 Fold the thread in half and holding the two ends in one hand, pass the loop over the forefinger of your other hand or over a pencil. Now rotate your finger until the thread begins to twist and resemble a cord.

3 Continue twisting the threads, holding the ends securely. Eventually the twisted thread will spring back on itself and you will have a silky smooth cord. Knot the loose ends securely to stop the threads unravelling, leaving enough thread to tease out into a tassel if desired

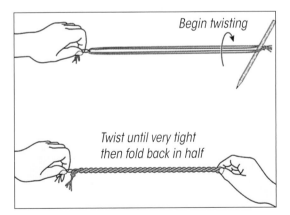

Fig 8 Making a length of twisted cord from embroidery threads

Making a Bell Pull

I used a linen band to make the dragon bell pull on page 93 but a 14-count Aida fabric band will work as well, stitched over one block instead of two linen threads. Alternatively, you could stitch the design on a piece of Aida or linen and hem all sides when the embroidery is finished. A wall hanging is made in a similar way.

You will need

☆ Iron-on interfacing, same size as finished embroidery

☆ Wooden bell pull rods and ends (see Suppliers)

☆ 1m (1yd) of cord for hanging

☆ Two tassels (optional)

1 Once the embroidery is finished trim it to the length required, allowing enough fabric to go over the bell pull rods at the top and bottom. Iron interfacing on to the back of the band to stiffen it slightly (see page 99).

2 Make a small turning at the top of the band and then fold it over the rod and sew to the back of the band with small slipstitches. Do the same at the bottom of the band.

3 Attach the tassels to the lower rod at either side of the band. I used ready-made tassels but you could make your own – see below. Finally, cut the length of cord in two and tie to each side of the upper rod to act as a hanger.

Making a Tassel

A tassel makes a nice finishing touch, for example on the corners of a cushion or sachet or at the end of a bookmark.

1 To make a simple tassel, cut an oblong piece of stiff card, about 1.5cm (½in) longer than the desired size of the tassel.

2 Choose a thread colour to match your project and wrap the thread around the card to the desired thickness.

3 Slip a length of thread through the top of the tassel and tie in a knot and then slide the threads off the card.

4 Bind the top third of the tassel with another length of thread and then trim all the tassel ends to the same length.

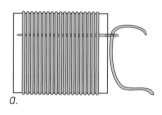

a.   b.   c.

Fig 9 Stages for making a tassel

Perfect Stitching

Counted cross stitch is one of the easiest forms of embroidery. Following these useful pointers when stitching the designs in this book will help you to produce neat and excellent work.

✫ Before starting, check the design size given with each project and make sure that this is the size you require for your finished embroidery.

✫ The fabric you are stitching on should be at least 5cm (2in) larger all round than the finished size of the stitching, to allow for making up.

✫ Organize your threads before you start a project as this will help to avoid confusion later. Put the threads required for a particular project on an organizer (available from craft shops) and always include the manufacturer's name and the shade number. You can easily make your own thread organizer by using a hole punch to punch holes along one side of a piece of thick card.

✫ When you have cut the length of stranded cotton (floss) you need, usually about 46cm (18in), separate out all the strands before taking the number you need, realigning them and threading your needle.

✫ When stitching with metallic threads, work with shorter lengths, about 30cm (12in) to avoid tangling and excessive wear on the thread.

Metallic threads are available in a glorious range of colours.

✫ If using a frame, try to avoid using a hoop as it can stretch the fabric and leave a mark that may be difficult to remove. If you do use a hoop, avoid placing it over worked stitches and remove it from the fabric at the end of a stitching session.

✫ Plan your route carefully around the chart, counting over short distances where possible to avoid making counting mistakes. Check your position against the chart frequently.

✫ Whenever possible, work your cross stitch in two directions in a sewing movement – half cross stitch in one direction and then cover those original stitches with the second row. This produces neat work and forms vertical lines on the back and gives somewhere to finish off raw ends tidily.

✫ For neat cross stitching, work the top stitches so they all face in the same direction.

✫ Avoid bringing the needle up through occupied holes from the back, where there is already a stitch, as you may pierce the stitch or snag it and spoil the existing stitch. Insert the needle from the front wherever possible.

✫ If your thread begins to twist, turn the work upside down every so often and let the needle spin, which will unwind the thread.

✫ Take care when turning your work to stitch different parts of a design – it is easy to inadvertently change the direction of the top stitch on your cross stitch and spoil the neat look of your work.

✫ If adding a backstitch outline, always add it after the cross stitch has been completed to prevent the solid line of the backstitch being broken.

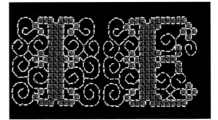

Backstitch can create very decorative effects and enhance a cross stitch design, especially if worked in a colour that contrasts well with the fabric.

Suppliers

Beadworks (UK)
21a Tower Street, Covent Garden, London WC2H 9NS, UK
Tel: 0208 553 3240
www.beadwork.co.uk
For beads and charms

Beadworks (USA)
167 Newberry Street, Boston, MA 02116, USA
Tel: 617 247 7227
www.boston@beadwork.com
For beads and charms

The Button Lady
16 Hollyfields South, Sutton Coldfield, West Midlands B76 1NX, UK
Tel: 01213 293 234
For buttons and charms

Coats Craft UK
PO Box 22, Lingfield Estate, McMullen Road, Darlington, County Durham DL1 1YQ, UK
Tel: 01325 3654579 (for a list of stockists)
For embroidery supplies and threads

DMC Creative World
Pullman Road, Wigston, Leicestershire LE18 2DY, UK
Tel: 0116 281 1040
Fax: 0116 281 3592
www.dmc/cw.com
For embroidery supplies and threads

Framecraft Miniatures Ltd
Isis House, Linden Road, Brownhills, West Midlands WS8 7BW, UK
Tel: 01543 360 842
Fax: 01543 453 154
Email: sales@framecraft.com
www.framecraft.com
For ready-made items with cross stitch inserts, including coasters, paperweights, bowls, pots, mirrors and pincushions

Heritage Stitchcraft
Redbrook Lane, Brereton, Rugeley, Staffordshire WS15 1QU, UK
Tel: +44 (0) 1889 575256
Email: enquiries@heritagestitchcraft.com
www.heritagestitchcraft.com
For cross stitch fabrics including Zweigart, bands, table linen and other embroidery supplies

Kreinik Manufacturing Company Inc
3106 Timanus Lane, Suite 101, Baltimore, MD 21244, USA
Tel: 1800 537 2166
Email: kreinik@kreinik.com
www.kreinik.com
For a wide range of metallic threads

Mill Hill, a division of Wichelt Imports Inc
N162 Hwy 35, Stoddard WI 54658, USA
Tel: 608 788 4600
Fax: 608 788 6040
Email: millhill@millhill.com
www. millhill.com
For Mill Hill beads and a US source for Framecraft products

The Viking Loom
22 High Petergate, York YO1 7EH, UK
Tel: 01904 765 599
www.vikingloom.co.uk
For bell pulls and linen bands

Zweigart / Joan Toggit Ltd
262 Old New Brunswick Road, Suite E, Piscataway, NJ 08854 03756, USA
Tel: 732 562 8888
Email: info@zweigart.com
www.zweigart.com
For cross stitch fabrics, bands and table linens

The Art and Framing Centre
Sudbury & Witham
76 North Street, Sudbury CO10 1RF, UK
Tel: 01787 310900
Email: artandframing@hotmail.com

Acknowledgments

With thanks to everyone at David & Charles, and especially Cheryl Brown for having the faith in me to suggest that *Fantasy Cross Stitch* should be my next book. It has been quite a journey but the most enjoyable and exciting undertaking. Thanks to Bethany Dymond my Desk Editor for keeping a check on me and Charly Bailey for the lovely page layouts and book design. A very special thank you goes to Lin Clements, who yet again has not only produced the beautiful charts for the book but edited the text in her usual thorough way to provide a wonderful end result.

I am grateful to Dena Lenham at Kreinik for the supply of beautiful metallic threads that are such a joy to stitch with. Thank you to Heritage Stitchcraft for all the linen and Aida fabrics and Becky Jackson at DMC for all the stranded cottons. Thanks also to Michael Oxley at The Art and Framing Centre in Sudbury, Suffolk, who has again done a superb job with all the framing.

And many thanks to a most important person, Tina Godwin, my stitcher, who has had to cope with tight deadlines and computer problems, plus supporting me throughout without a cross word – my love and thanks. To Angela Ottewell who stitched the designs for the Native American Birth Totems chapter through an especially difficult time for her – thank you. And to Rosemary, who is always there to give a helping hand.

About the Author

Lesley Teare

Lesley trained as a textile designer, with a degree in printed and woven textiles. For some years she has been one of DMC's leading designers and her designs have also featured in many of the cross stitch magazines. Lesley has contributed to five other books for David & Charles, *Cross Stitch Greetings Cards*, *Cross Stitch Alphabets*, *Cross Stitch Angels*, *Cross Stitch Fairies* and *Magical Cross Stitch*. Her book *101 Weekend Cross Stitch Gifts* was followed by *Travel the World in Cross Stitch* and then *Oriental Cross Stitch*. Lesley lives in Hitcham, Suffolk.

Index